The Country Wife

THE NEW MERMAIDS

General editor: Brian Gibbons
Professor of English Literature, University of Münster

THE NEW MERMAIDS

The Country Wife

WILLIAM WYCHERLEY

Edited by

JAMES OGDEN

Senior Lecturer in English
University College of Wales, Aberystwyth

LONDON / A & C BLACK

NEW YORK / W W NORTON

Second edition 1991
Reprinted 1991, 1992, 1993, 1994
by A & C Black (Publishers) Limited
35 Bedford Row, London WC1R 4JH
ISBN 0-7136-3287-9

© *1991 A & C Black (Publishers) Limited*

First published in this form 1973
by Ernest Benn Limited
© *1973 Ernest Benn Limited*

Published in the United States of America by
W. W. Norton & Company Inc.
500 Fifth Avenue, New York, N.Y. 10110
ISBN 0-393-90063-0

A CIP catalogue record for this book
is available from the British Library
and the Library of Congress.

Printed in Great Britain by
Whitstable Litho Printers Ltd,
Whitstable, Kent

CONTENTS

TO ARTHUR SCOUTEN

ACKNOWLEDGEMENTS

Most of the work on this edition was done in Aberystwyth. I am grateful to the University College of Wales for granting me a term's study leave, and to members of the English Department, the Hugh Owen Library, and the National Library of Wales – especially my colleagues Peter Bement, Mike Smith, Richard Brinkley and Ron Job – for help in various ways. I also spent some time in Cambridge University Library, where I was assisted by Elizabeth Erskine and Brian Jenkins. I am deeply indebted to previous editors, especially John Dixon Hunt, the late Thomas Fujimura, Gerald Weales, David Cook and John Swannell, Arthur Friedman, and Peter Holland. Some acknowledgement of these debts is made in the notes. Correspondents who gave useful advice and encouragement were Arthur Scouten, Edward Langhans, Stuart Sillars, Frank Lamport, and of course the general editor of the New Mermaids, Brian Gibbons. For the publishers, Anne Watts and Margaret Parker helped me to deal with problems of presentation. Mrs Jean Cock did an excellent job on the typescript.

JAMES OGDEN

INTRODUCTION

THE AUTHOR

WYCHERLEY WOULD KNOW that the true poet 'ought himself to be a true poem', as Milton put it,[1] but his life compared with his plays seems shapeless; certainly we lack information to see a pattern, but perhaps he lacked power to create one.

At the time of Wycherley's birth, his family had been living in Shropshire for two centuries or more, and their estate at Clive was worth about £600 a year.[2] His father, Daniel Wycherley, had become steward to the Marquess of Winchester; his mother, Bethia Shrimpton, had been an attendant to the Marchioness. William was probably born on 28 March 1641, and he was baptised at Whitchurch, Hampshire, on 8 April that year. Daniel Wycherley was an able man, who inherited the family estate and increased its value, but became so engrossed in lawsuits as to prefigure Dickens's 'Man from Shropshire' in *Bleak House*. Bethia Shrimpton, 'who if she wanted beauty had a large share of tongue', was another strong character, though much of her time would be spent in domesticity and childbearing; there were three sons and two daughters after William.[3]

Daniel looked after his eldest son's education, and in 1656 William was sent to France to join the *précieux* salon of Madame de Montausier at Angoulême. Here he was converted to Roman Catholicism, and would meet many who were prominent in French life, including the Marquis de Montausier, who has been seen as the original of Alceste in Molière's *Le Misanthrope*, and

---

[1] *An Apology against a Pamphlet* (1641). Ben Jonson had remarked on 'the impossibility of any man's being the good poet, without first being a good man' in the prefatory epistle to *Volpone* (1607).

[2] Richardson Pack, 'Memoirs of Mr. Wycherley's Life', in Wycherley's *Posthumous Works*, ed. Lewis Theobald (1728), p. 5. G.E. Aylmer, *The King's Servants* (Routledge, 1974), p. 331, estimates average annual income for 1633: peers, £6000; knights, £800; esquires, £500; gentlemen, £150.

[3] The standard biography is B. Eugene McCarthy's *William Wycherley* (Ohio University Press, 1979), but for Wycherley's birth see Friedman, pp. xiii-xiv footnote, and for his mother see Richard Gough, *The History of Myddle*, ed. David Hey (Penguin, 1981), p. 140.

so perhaps of Manly in Wycherley's *The Plain Dealer*. Shortly before the Restoration he returned to England; he was admitted to the Inner Temple, London, in 1659, and went to Queen's College, Oxford, in 1660. At Oxford he probably reverted to Protestantism, but he did not matriculate. He was soon back in London leading the life of a fashionable gentleman and aspiring courtier, which included occasional military service. He was in Ireland with the Earl of Arran's regiment in 1662, he probably served at sea in the Second Dutch War in 1665, and he was made a Captain in the Duke of Buckingham's regiment in 1672.

Meanwhile Wycherley's literary career began with occasional poems and the anonymous publication of *Hero and Leander in Burlesque* in 1669. His first two plays, *Love in a Wood* and *The Gentleman Dancing-Master*, were performed in 1671 and 1672, the former by the King's Company at the Bridges Street theatre, the latter by the Duke's at Dorset Garden. There is a story that the success of *Love in a Wood* and the handsome appearance of its author excited Charles II's ex-mistress Barbara Villiers, Lady Castlemaine, and that Wycherley became one of her lovers. Certainly the King himself 'was extremely fond of him upon account of his wit',[4] and he became friendly with Buckingham and other courtiers. With the performances by the King's Company at Drury Lane of *The Country Wife* in 1675 and *The Plain Dealer* in 1676 he established himself as the leading writer of satirical comedy. The success of the latter owed something to the 'loud approbation' of his aristocratic friends, and led to his becoming known after its principal character as 'the Plain Dealer' or 'Manly'. Dryden summarised these impressions when he referred to 'the satire, wit, and strength of manly Wycherley'.[5]

As Wycherley lived almost another forty years, but did not write another play, the rest of his life makes depressing reading. He suffered various misfortunes, and made numerous mistakes. In 1677 he was seriously ill with a fever which undermined his health and affected his memory. King Charles visited him at his lodgings, paid for a convalescence abroad, and later made him tutor to his bastard son the Duke of Richmond at a salary of £1500 a year. But meanwhile the temperamental Countess of Drogheda had fallen for Wycherley, and on the death of her husband in June 1679 they secretly married; when Charles got to hear about it, Wycherley lost favour.

Wycherley's wife was a financial liability, as she had personal

---

[4]   Pack (note 2), p. 8
[5]   'To my Dear Friend Mr. Congreve' (1694)

debts, and her late husband's will was contested by the family. When she died in 1685 her will was contested by the family too, and Wycherley was involved in seemingly endless lawsuits, just like his father. Soon he was committed to the Fleet Prison for debts amounting to over £1500. He asked his friend the Earl of Mulgrave for help, and Mulgrave apparently arranged a court performance of *The Plain Dealer* before the new king, James II. James liked the play, and perhaps the playwright pleased him further by professing his Roman Catholicism; anyway Wycherley was released, presented with £500, and granted an annual pension of £200; and these kindnesses 'made Mr Wycherley always a Jacobite'.[6] But of course when James lost his throne, Wycherley lost his pension. His financial problems and associated lawsuits continued at least until the death of his father and his inheritance of Clive Hall in 1697.

Wycherley's literary achievements, civilised manners, and witty conversation enabled him to retain the respect of the younger men of letters who gathered at Will's Coffee House near his London lodgings. He announced the publication of his miscellaneous *Poems*, but it was some eight years before they appeared in 1704, and the poems themselves were unworthy of him, as he partly knew. At about this time Alexander Pope sought his friendship to enter the literary world, and Wycherley got Pope's help to revise the poems.

Pope says Wycherley told him he would not marry again till he was on his deathbed, and Wycherley was certainly dying when he married Elizabeth Jackson on 20 December 1715. She was supposed to be an heiress, but was in fact the mistress of his unscrupulous cousin Thomas Shrimpton. At the time of the marriage Wycherley also received Extreme Unction according to the Roman Catholic rite; Pope joked about the sequence of sacraments and recorded Wycherley's humorous advice to his wife, 'Never marry an old man again'.[7] Wycherley died on New Year's Eve and was buried at St Paul's, Covent Garden; Shrimpton married his widow, and after more litigation took control of his estate. It is a sad irony that the dramatist's life should have ended with such farcical scenes.

[6]   Charles Gildon, *Memoirs of the Life of William Wycherley* (1718), pp. 7–8
[7]   Letter from Pope to Edward Blount, 21 January 1715/16, in *The Corre-spondence of Alexander Pope*, ed. George Sherburn (Oxford, 1956), vol. 1, pp. 328–9. See also H.P. Vincent, 'The Death of William Wycherley', *Harvard Studies and Notes*, vol. 15 (1933), 219–42.

THE PLAY

Our scene is London; the time, 1675. The characters appear in the elaborate costume of Restoration ladies and gentlemen before familiar scenes of fashionable lodgings, houses, and places of resort. They speak mainly in prose; which, as we may know, Molière's *bourgeois gentilhomme* found to his surprise he had been doing all his life.[8] That is to say, while their speech is stylised and theatrical – allowing them memorable witticisms, pointed asides, good exit lines, and couplets at the ends of the Acts – it is only what we Restoration ladies and gentlemen ourselves aspire to; Sparkish even claims that some of us 'speak more wit' than the silly rogues who write our plays (III. ii. 98–100). But as life does not throw up eccentric characters and farcical situations with such regularity, we scarcely suppose we are being given a realistic view of it, and we may be transported into a purely theatrical world. For audiences today, this effect may be reinforced by the costumes and scenery of a remote and incredible period; yet the temptation to escape into fantasy should be resisted. If we can see the characters and situations as exaggerating those of ordinary life for the sake of satirical comedy, the play will make us think as well as laugh.

The Country Wife has three nicely related plots. Its opening lines introduce the first, in which the rakish Horner pretends to be a eunuch, fools Sir Jaspar Fidget and Lady Squeamish, and so manages to have sex with Lady Fidget and probably Mrs Dainty Fidget and Mrs Squeamish as well. This 'virtuous gang, as they call themselves' (V.ii.96) finally returns to Horner's lodgings and boasts of having had him. In the second plot, the country wife comes to town and wants to enjoy all its pleasures, especially that of being loved by Horner; her husband, Pinchwife, knows nothing of the feigned impotence, does all he can to be avoid being cuckolded, but only makes sure that he is. In the third plot, Horner's friend Harcourt successfully woos Pinchwife's sister, Alithea, away from her proposed husband, Sparkish.

It is all over in a few hours in the theatre, and is supposed to be all over in two days in real life. The first three Acts take place on the first day, and the last two on the second. The first Act is set at Horner's lodgings late in the morning (I.i.114–15). The second is set at Pinchwife's house early in the afternoon (most people are about to go to a play). The third begins there

---

[8] Molière, *Le Bourgeois Gentilhomme* II.iv, in *Oeuvres Complètes*, ed. Georges Couton (Gallimard, 1971), vol. 2, p. 730

early in the evening (the play is over) and moves to the New Exchange a little later (the shops are still open). Now, in a modern production, we expect the interval. The fourth Act begins at Pinchwife's house on the morning of the next day (Alithea is preparing for her marriage to Sparkish before noon). The scene changes to Horner's lodgings early in the afternoon (the marriage is supposed to have taken place, and Sparkish invites people to dinner). Scenes between the Pinchwifes proceed simultaneously, and by Act V it is evening (candles are needed). The scene at Covent Garden takes place in semi-darkness ('*Enter* ALITHEA *following a torch*', V.iii.23). The final scene takes place at night, when Horner has bedded Mrs Pinchwife, though it is not too late for everybody to come to his lodgings for various reasons.[9] Obviously, the long scenes of the first three acts and the short ones of the last two create an impression of events rushing to a climax. Less obviously, the effect of the play beginning at Horner's lodgings, moving to Pinchwife's house and other locations, and ending back at Horner's is to suggest that the Horner plot is primary, the Pinchwife plot is secondary, and the Harcourt-Alithea-Sparkish plot is anywhere or nowhere.

The Country Wife has been and remains controversial. In its time it has been admired as a satire or farce, condemned as an immoral or frivolous play, and admired again as a serious work of dramatic art. Modern critics have wanted to show that it has unity – unity being the one criterion of merit that is generally accepted – so they have identified central themes: female hypocrisy, true and false masculinity, human folly in general, to name only three. Disagreements between these critics can perhaps be settled by arguing that such themes are all present, but none is absolutely central; yet more serious disagreements remain over attitudes to Horner. Is he the satire's hero and vehicle, or its villain and target? Is he the man we dream we could be or could have, or the man we fear we really are or have got? And unfortunately answers to these questions do not fully resolve others, such as how sorry we can feel for the Pinchwifes, or how happy for the Harcourts.[10]

But it is best to begin with Horner. He plans to fool everybody, especially the husbands, keepers, and guardians of

9   For a more detailed time and scene plan, see Judith Milhous and Robert D. Hume, *Producible Interpretation* (Southern Illinois University Press, 1985), pp. 104–6.

10 The history of Wycherley criticism in general is surveyed by B. Eugene McCarthy, *William Wycherley: A Reference Guide* (G.K. Hall, 1985), and of *Country Wife* criticism in particular by Milhous and Hume (note 9).

attractive women; and to seduce the women, foreseeing that those who are disgusted by a eunuch will be fascinated by a rake. His assistant, Quack, thinks the scheme crazy, and we may think there are not many men who would sacrifice all public respect for such private satisfactions. He cannot even confide in his friends Harcourt and Dorilant. They discuss the relative merits of mistresses and fellowship, and Horner comes to the memorable conclusion:

> For my part I will have only those glorious, manly pleasures of being very drunk and very slovenly. (I.i.238–9)

But this is thoroughly disingenuous; he does not mean to confine himself to those pleasures, and really associates slovenliness with the miseries of marriage (ll.360–2). When Sparkish comes to mock Horner's impotence, his friends combine to mock Sparkish's witlessness, but they do not know that the impotence is feigned. So our first impression of Horner – and first impressions are vital in the theatre – is that he is with the wits but not of them, not only clever and cynical, but also detached and sinister.

And yet we should not be determined to prove Horner a villain, as there are no real villainies for him to commit. His first victim, Sir Jaspar Fidget, is sometimes seen as 'Wycherley's portrait of a new brand of business entrepreneur'.[11] I wish he were, but the truth is that the 'business' that busies him is at court; on his first appearance he is on the way to a Privy Council meeting, or wants to give that impression (I.i.115–16), and later he says he has been 'advancing a certain project to his majesty' (III.ii.570). As his name implies, he is 'a fidgeting, busy, dogmatical, hot-headed fop', the character of 'a politic wit' in *Love in a Wood,* and a descendant of Sir Politick Would-be in *Volpone,*[12] not a new brand of businessman at all. Both Sir

---

Critics who have identified central themes include Kenneth Muir, *The Comedy of Manners* (Hutchinson, 1970): 'the main force of Wycherley's satire is directed against female hypocrisy' (p. 76); David M. Vieth, 'Wycherley's *The Country Wife:* An Anatomy of Masculinity', *Papers on Language and Literature,* vol. 2 (1966), 335–50; and R. Edgley, 'The Object of Literary Criticism', *Essays in Criticism,* vol. 14 (1964), 221–36: 'the direct topic of criticism in *The Country Wife* is folly'. Milhous and Hume conclude that, 'given the wide-open nature of the script, and the broad range of production concepts appropriate to it, to imagine that there is a single "valid" interpretation is madness' (p. 104).

[11] W.R. Chadwick, *The Four Plays of William Wycherley* (Mouton, 1975), p. 105

[12] See the notes on 'Persons in the Play' (p. 4) and on I.i.115, 116.

Jaspar and Sir Politick are obsessed with their projects and neglectful of their wives, though only Sir Jaspar is cuckolded, and he is soon persuaded that he has not been. We do not grudge Horner the satisfaction of duping this pompous fool.

It is debatable whether the virtuous gang are Horner's victims, or *vice-versa*. At first Lady Fidget and Dainty seem comic characters like Sir Jaspar; as they find Horner's pretence of misogyny bad enough, but that of impotence even worse, they begin to prove him right in thinking that women who show an aversion to him really love the sport. Then, for an episode in Act II which is not required by the plot, the gang is joined by Mrs Squeamish, turns out in full force against Pinchwife, and drives him from his own reception room. Lady Fidget leads this outrageous assembly in revealing the lusts behind the cloak of virtue:

> To report a man has had a person, when he has not had a person, is the greatest wrong in the whole world that can be done to a person. (II.i.386–8)

Sir Jaspar re-introduces Horner, who now feels he knows Lady Fidget well enough to 'venture with her, my secret for hers' (ll. 543–4). The exchange made, she anticipates the greatest good in her whole world, to have it reported that a man has not had a person, when he has:

> But, poor gentleman, could you be so generous, so truly a man of honour, as for the sakes of us women of honour, to cause yourself to be reported no man? No man! And to suffer yourself the greatest shame that could fall upon a man, that none might fall upon us women by your conversation? (ll. 555–60)

Her idea is that a man's greatest shame would be to be reported as a eunuch, and his greatest triumph not to be suspected as a lecher. It is expressed in a mixture of courtly language and sexual suggestion that soon produces comic effects:

HORNER
> I desire to be tried only, madam.

LADY FIDGET
> Well, that's spoken again like a man of honour; all men of honour desire to come to the test. (ll. 564–6)

When she comes to his lodgings to bring him to the test she takes the initiative with a pun on his name and her favourite word – 'Well, Horner, am I not a woman of honour?' (IV.iii.38) – and holds her own in the inevitable verbal fencing:

HORNER
> To talk of honour in the mysteries of love is like talking of heaven or the deity in an operation of witchcraft, just when you are employing the devil; it makes the charm impotent.

LADY FIDGET
> Nay, fie, let us not be smutty. (ll. 46–50)

Critics who suppose she cannot see the funny side of such remarks credit her with no sense of humour. When Sir Jaspar interrupts, she takes control; she contrives to have sex with Horner under her husband's nose, to re-enter with a piece of china or phallic symbol,[13] and to express satisfaction without being smutty:

LADY FIDGET
> I have been toiling and moiling for the prettiest piece of china, my dear.

HORNER
> Nay, she has been too hard for me, do what I could. (ll.187–9)

Here Mrs Squeamish decides 'I'll have some china too'. We have been told at the opening of the scene that people like Sir Jaspar and old Lady Squeamish think Horner 'as unfit for love as they are', but their wives, sisters, and daughters know better; so we should expect Dainty Fidget and Mrs Squeamish to want their share of him. The famous china scene is funny however it is played, but funniest I think assuming only Sir Jaspar does not know what they are talking about:

SQUEAMISH
> Good Master Horner, don't think to give other people china, and me none. Come in with me too.

HORNER
> Upon my honour I have none left now... This lady had the last there.

LADY FIDGET
> Yes indeed, madam, to my certain knowledge he has no more left.

SQUEAMISH
> Oh, but it may be he may have some you could not find.

LADY FIDGET
> What, d'ye think if he had any left, I would not have had it too? For we women of quality never think we have china enough.
> (ll.190–202)

But soon Horner is promising china to Mrs Squeamish 'another

---

[13] See the note on IV.iii.204.

time', Lady Fidget is taking a jealous interest in their conversation, and his explanation that Mrs Squeamish 'has an innocent, literal understanding' (l.207) does not convince.[14]

The final appearance of the virtuous gang is another scene which is necessary for the satire rather than the plot. By Act V they have made Horner's lodgings their hideout, and he has to drink with them with a vengeance. Inspired by the wine, they acknowledge that their virtue is a disguise:

> Our reputation! Lord, why should you not think that we women make use of our reputation, as you men of yours, only to deceive the world with less suspicion? Our virtue is like the statesman's religion, the Quaker's word, the gamester's oath, and the great man's honour – but to cheat those that trust us. (V.iv.102–7)

This speech outgoes Horner in cynicism. Critics have felt that the drunken women are so disgusting that the focus of satire shifts from their affectations to their beastliness,[15] and there is certainly something alarming about them in this mood. But a major effect of the scene is the embarrassment of Horner, who never expected anything like it. He finds himself obliged to confess the beastliness of his own activities:

> Ceremony in love and eating is as ridiculous as in fighting. Falling on briskly is all should be done on those occasions. (ll. 88–90)

Love means sex, and they all know that sex means falling on briskly. Lady Fidget immediately says women 'think wildness in a man as desirable a quality as in a duck or rabbit' (ll. 97–8). Yet she claims Horner as her own, so Mrs Squeamish and Dainty Fidget claim him too. The gang who first affected virtue, then discussed sex in code, now make plausible claims that they have all had it with Horner. And in the bedroom there is Mrs Pinchwife, who will soon escape and try to tell everyone he is hers. A man who has apparently had four women in one day can hardly avoid being an object of ridicule himself.

Another comic aspect of Horner's situation is that he can attract cuckolds and women without pretending to be a eunuch. Jack Pinchwife is an old rake who has married a country girl because, as he admits, 'I could never keep a whore to myself' (I.i.461–2). He thinks he can keep his wife to himself by locking her up or threatening violence. If he sometimes seems a clown, he often seems a tyrant; to modern audiences he will

---

[14] See the note on IV.iii.205–7.
[15] Especially Rose A. Zimbardo, *Wycherley's Drama: A Link in the Development of English Satire* (Yale, 1965), pp. 147–53

probably seem a monster. Unlike Sir Jaspar, he knows nothing of the feigned impotence and has no project to employ Horner; but he is strangely attracted to him, appearing at his lodgings for no reason, arousing his interest in Mrs Pinchwife despite himself. He feels fated to play the cuckold's part, and is grimly aware that cuckolds 'are generally makers of their own fortune' (III.i.58–9). Those who have read their Freud[16] will see him as a neurotic character, his own worst enemy, and pathetic if you think about him. Certainly the inner life of such a man must be a mess, but Pinchwife is given few chances to win sympathy. Typically, when he threatens to murder his wife she scarcely takes him seriously, and Sparkish enters to make a joke of it (IV.iv.42–9). Perhaps at the end, struggling for his own peace of mind to believe he has not been cuckolded, he is a sad case.

Margery Pinchwife's naïveté is so exaggerated in the early scenes that she seems a caricature of the country innocent. She twice says she has no idea what jealousy is, treats her monstrous husband as if he were a child, and seems to think him capable only of petty nastiness. Her simplicity gives her charm, however, so she can be seen as showing there are better ways of behaving than those of the town, or as being corrupted by the town's values. With the help of her mad husband and her artful maid she finds her way to Horner's bed, but naïvely supposes they can get rid of her husband and live together, and is therefore ready to tell everyone they are lovers. Has she learnt nothing at all? Well, she has ceased to long for the country, and has learned to 'loathe, nauseate, and detest' her husband (IV.iv.24). Her marriage is plainly no joke, and it may be that at the end of the play the comic balance is best preserved if she seems to have at least some hope of diversion. What does Dorilant tell her that keeps her quiet? He for his part is finally more impressed by the bad example of the Pinchwifes than by the good one of Harcourt and Alithea, so he resolves not to marry; but perhaps he has resolved to keep Mrs Pinchwife.

Harcourt and Alithea's marriage can be said to show a better way of life than Horner and Dorilant's rakish careers.[17] Alithea's critical attitude to the Pinchwifes' marriage establishes her as a sensible character, though she is herself betrothed to Sparkish. This foppish courtier and would-be wit 'can no more think the

---

[16] For example Norman Holland, *The First Modern Comedies* (Harvard, 1959), pp. 73–5

[17] An interpretation proposed by Holland (note 16) and supported with reservations by Anne Righter, 'William Wycherley', *Restoration Theatre*, ed. John Russell Brown and Bernard Harris (Arnold, 1965), pp. 70–91

men laugh at him than that women jilt him, his opinion of himself is so good' (I.i.243–4). Alithea is not unaware of his failings but remains faithful, trying to believe his toleration of Harcourt proves his love for her. He is certainly no Pinchwife, but only because he thinks jealousy unfashionable and finds her unattractive. Harcourt's intrigues delay the proposed marriage till other intrigues prevent it; having seen the letter Alithea is supposed to have sent to Horner, Sparkish rounds on her:

> I never had any passion for you till now, for now I hate you. 'Tis true I might have married your portion, as other men of parts of the town do sometimes; and so your servant. And to show my unconcernedness, I'll come to your wedding and resign you with as much joy as I would a stale wench to a new cully. (V.iii.69–75)

So Sparkish's nasty nature is glimpsed behind his engaging foppery. The way is almost open for Alithea to marry Harcourt, but first he must prove himself a true lover. After all, he belongs to what she calls the society of the wits, and can talk like a libertine:

> Mistresses are like books; if you pore upon them too much they doze you and make you unfit for company, but if used discreetly you are the fitter for conversation by 'em. (I.i.214–17)

Worse, he habitually confuses courting Alithea with procuring a mistress, as in this aside about taking advantage of Sparkish:

> So we are hard put to't, when we make our rival our procurer; but... when all's done, a rival is the best cloak to steal to a mistress under. (III.ii.187–90)

Maybe she is right to fear that all men of the town make bad husbands. She deduces from Pinchwife's case that they are prone to jealousy and so to incarcerating their wives in the country, a fate almost worse than death (IV.i.56–67). She sees through Harcourt's intrigues and finds his love ridiculous and troublesome (ll. 141, 145). So there is some excuse for the episode in Act V where Horner, trying to keep Pinchwife in the dark, pretends there really is something between himself and Alithea. She cannot clear her name, so Harcourt steps forward:

> Madam... you shall now see 'tis possible for me to love too, without being jealous. I will not only believe your innocence myself, but make all the world believe it. (V.iv.262–5)

If we like, we can say they are now well matched, as she appreciates his superiority to Sparkish in both wit and worth, and he supports his romantic talk with a chivalrous gesture.

But probably we will feel more critical. As Sparkish is at best a fool, how can Alithea be both sensible about life and serious about him? It is absurd to prefer Sparkish merely because Harcourt unsettles her wedding plans; indeed worse than absurd, as Lucy points out:

> Can there be a greater cheat or wrong done to a man than to give him your person without your heart? I should make a conscience of it. (IV.i.19–21)

Her brother thinks she wants Sparkish because she loves all the follies of the town; it may be worrying to have Pinchwife on our side, but we may well notice that her final acceptance of Harcourt does not dissociate her from town values, that she originally took Horner of all people for a man of honour (V.iv.250–1), and that even when she knows what he is she urbanely supports the efforts to whitewash him. 'Come brother', she says to Pinchwife, 'your wife is yet innocent you see' (l. 394). But above all what makes the Harcourt-Alithea-Sparkish plot unacceptable as the play's moral centre is that the other plots put it in the shade. And it is no good saying moral heroes and heroines are always outshone by immoral ones. Alithea and Harcourt might have been given the positive significance of Millamant and Mirabel in *The Way of the World*; but they have not, because Wycherley was a more sceptical writer than Congreve.

Would a Restoration audience have been more inclined than we are to accept Alithea uncritically? They would have been less likely to find her attitude to town and country unbalanced. And they would have been more aware of the predicament of young unmarried women at the time: they were expected to take the husbands their parents or guardians chose for them. Pinchwife has accepted Sparkish's offer to take Alithea off his hands for £5000. The advice given to women in such a situation was to make the best of it; which perhaps is what Alithea tries to do, even hoping love will follow marriage, though Lucy puts her right here (IV.i.23–7). Of course Wycherley knew these arranged marriages often worked badly, so we can infer that he was attacking them. And of course the Pinchwife and Fidget marriages are deplorable, so the satire on the whole institution by Horner and the wits is understandable. Still, the alternative is represented not by an admirable marriage but by a farcical courtship; compared with Millamant and Mirabel, Alithea and Harcourt tell us nothing about what the marriage of true minds might be like.

The effect, and surely also the point, of juxtaposing these

three plots is to suggest that foolish or vicious men always lose their women to intelligent or virtuous ones. The foolish or vicious men – and women, as Wycherley throws in Old Lady Squeamish at the end – should present few problems for directors, audiences, or even critics. Broad similarities are clear. Sir Jaspar, believing Horner impotent and Lady Fidget virtuous, makes them companions and is cuckolded. Pinchwife, believing Horner lecherous and Margery naïve, brings them together by trying to keep them apart, and he is cuckolded too. Sparkish, believing Harcourt his friend and Alithea his property, shows her off to him and is jilted. All three fail to see that their women are capable of independent thought and action; hence these foolish or vicious men are almost wholly objects of satire. Of course there are interesting differences. Sir Jaspar is silly, harmless, and self-assured, where Pinchwife and Sparkish are relatively shrewd, vicious, and vulnerable. These two are to be contrasted, the one madly jealous and the other madly complaisant. Sparkish is engaging enough till his vicious streak appears in his showdown with Alithea. Pinchwife's real feelings are always near the surface, inclining him to violence. He may seem fated to be a cuckold, and in that way sympathetic; but the possibility of perverse and vicarious satisfactions in his role is suggested, as it is more comically in the case of Old Lady Squeamish. She actually makes her daughter kiss Horner, and thrills at the thought of debauchery: 'Oh thou harloting harlotry! Hast thou done 't then?' (V.iv.320).

The intelligent or virtuous men do present problems. Some critics want Horner to be a Lawrentian life-force and prophet of the permissive society. Others make the obvious comparison with Harcourt, to conclude that Horner is vice and Harcourt is virtue.[18] The two heroes undoubtedly differ from their dupes, and perhaps from Dorilant too, in knowing that women cannot be treated as objects. Dorilant entertains, or is entertained by, straightforward male chauvinism:

A mistress should be like a little country retreat near the town; not to dwell in constantly, but only for a night and away, to taste the town the better when a man returns.　　　(I.i.218–21)

[18] For enthusiastic responses to Horner see C.D. Cecil, 'Libertine and Précieux Elements in Restoration Comedy', Essays in Criticism, vol. 9 (1959), 239–53, and Virginia Ogden Birdsall, Wild Civility (Indiana University Press, 1970): Horner represents 'the life force triumphant' (p. 156). For the idea that Harcourt and Horner represent right and wrong behaviour, see Holland (note 16) and Righter (note 17).

Horner is likewise for keeping a mistress against supporting a wife, but he is interested in intelligent women and stable relationships:

> Methinks wit is more necessary than beauty; and I think no young women ugly that has it, and no handsome woman agreeable without it. (ll. 425–7)
> Women ... are like soldiers, made constant and loyal by good pay rather than by oaths and covenants. (ll. 464–6)

And by good pay he means good sex. Harcourt romantically favours marriage against keeping; indeed he holds what remains today the most widely accepted idea of the good life. But the comparison between the two men is not exactly in his favour. Harcourt is less witty and amusing; and some of the respect he wins for his romantic idealism he loses through his farcical intrigue. He does not think his friend vicious; and neither should we. Horner commits no rapes or heartless seductions, but merely accepts the women who keep coming. The virtuous gang can even be seen as taking advantage of him. His most serious mistake is to suppose Margery Pinchwife will share his uncomplicated view of sex; this leads to more embarrassments in Act V. His most serious limitation is to live in a world of his own. He has respect for his friends, but cannot confide in them; he will do what he can to help Harcourt win Alithea, but if necessary he will fight him and injure her, to protect his own secret amours. In the end he may well strike us as a man for whom sex has become a ridiculous obsession.

Critics who like neat oppositions of vice and virtue will also find them among the women. Perhaps the neatest idea is that Lady Fidget is vice, Alithea is virtue, and Margery is the happy medium.[19] But Lady Fidget and Alithea are not wholly dissimilar. They are both town women and they both talk a lot about honour; they differ in the degree to which they allow it to influence their lives, Lady Fidget superficially and Alithea excessively. Lady Fidget's hypocrisy almost insinuates her into an affair with Horner, while Alithea's honour almost traps her into a marriage with Sparkish. Alithea is saved by her own good sense, the persistence of Harcourt, and the accidental exposure of Sparkish. Lady Fidget is thwarted by her own extravagance, the fickleness of Horner, and the drunken confessions of the virtuous gang. She has to share him with them. Compared

---

[19] Birdsall (note 18) makes Margery the 'heroine' because she is neither idealistic like Alithea nor hypocritical like Lady Fidget, but 'on the side of the instincts' (pp. 147–50).

with the town ladies, Margery lacks the dubious advantages of sophisticated education, and offers the real attractions of animal vitality. But she is no happy medium; she understands only her own feelings, conspicuously not those of her husband or her lover. At the end, a semblance of order is restored when the gang and Alithea make out that nobody has been cuckolded, but Margery, having learnt something of intrigue but nothing of discretion, would blurt out the truth but for Dorilant's intervention. As Lady Fidget says – aside to Horner – 'This you get, and we too, by trusting your secret to a fool' (V.iv.388–9).

The play, like others in the Jonsonian tradition of satirical comedy, does not so much recommend some modes of behaviour and denounce others as reveal what life is like and leave us to draw our own conclusions. And the life *The Country Wife* reveals is not unfamiliar. The world has its full complement of fools like Sir Jaspar, Sparkish, and Pinchwife; they may not be merely ridiculous, but they cannot be sympathetic, as their attitudes to women are so deplorable. The women are not such fools, though most of them are so repressed by convention or force that when they break loose they will stop at nothing to have sex. Horner accepts this situation realistically and plays the Don Juan. We may say that despite his realism he does not avoid becoming an object of satire himself; but we must admit that he gets away with it. The ideas that, like Volpone, he is becoming no more than his name implies and needs 'new tricks' to retain an interest in life keep coming to mind; but the alternative ideas, that he is an engaging scamp, or even a man with a philosophy from whom something is to be learned, will not go away. No doubt some women are more balanced than Horner's, so some happy marriages are possible, though the marriages we see in the play, those of the Fidgets and Pinchwifes, mix farce and tragedy. If we can suppose that the romantic marriage of Harcourt and Alithea will succeed, and that the lively improvisations of Horner and Margery will continue, our final impression will not be wholly pessimistic, though it may be purely personal.

SOURCES

Wycherley's most obvious debts are to Molière's *L'École des Maris* (1661) and *L'École des Femmes* (1662).[20] These comedies focus on the madness of men who will base marriage on the

[20] In Molière, *Oeuvres Complètes* (note 8), vol. 2

ignorance and servility of women; hence they are sources for the Pinchwife plot in particular.

In *L'École des Maris* the brothers Sganarelle and Ariste want to marry their wards, the sisters Isabelle and Léonor; Sganarelle's repressive treatment of Isabelle alienates her, but Ariste's liberal attitude towards Léonor wins her affection. Isabelle manages to convince Sganarelle that she loves him while making him her go-between with her lover, Valère. Sganarelle decides to marry her immediately, so she pretends Léonor has an assignation with Valère, and passes herself off as her sister; Sganarelle thinks he can now show Ariste the folly of liberality, and arranges the marriage of Valère and the supposed Léonor. But the real Léonor declares her love for Ariste, and when he sees what has happened Sganarelle can only 'renonce à jamais, à ce sexe trompeur'.

For *The Country Wife* Wycherley borrows the general idea of comparing repressive and liberal attitudes to women, but neither Pinchwife's repression nor Sparkish's liberality has the desired effect. He also borrows the particular device of making the victim the go-between. Isabelle tricks Sganarelle first into giving Valère a hint of her feelings, then into taking him a love letter, and finally into arranging their marriage. The Pinchwife plot develops similarly, but Margery is not as clever as Isabelle, and Pinchwife is more the victim of his own madness than Sganarelle. Isabelle's pretence that she is Léonor, to get into Valère's house, and her later apology to her sister (III.ix.1–2), probably suggested Margery's pretence that she is Alithea, to get into Horner's lodging, and her later apology to her sister-in-law (V.iv.295). Two further borrowings are worth noting. The sensible advice of Léonor and her servant, Lisette, to Sganarelle against his repressive behaviour (I.ii.133–60) probably inspired that of Alithea to Pinchwife against his (II.i.37–55), though Molière has set speeches where Wycherley has lively dialogue. And the scene in which Isabelle uses *double entendre* to deceive Sganarelle and assure Valère of her love (II.ix) broadly resembles episodes between Alithea, Harcourt, and Sparkish (II.i and III.ii), though in these Harcourt is the master of ambiguity, Sparkish is deceived, and Alithea is not wholly assured.

Wycherley's debts to *L'École des Femmes* are greater. In this play Arnolphe, a middle-aged man famous for his ridicule of cuckolds, plans to avoid being cuckolded himself by marrying his ward, Agnes, a girl he has brought up in a convent in complete ignorance. But she is so ignorant that she has no sense of obligation to him, and falls in love with Horace, the son of his friend Oronte. Although the lovers innocently confide in Arnolphe himself, he cannot prevent their eventual marriage. Again the main point of the play is the folly and wickedness of trying to achieve marriage by force.

Wycherley has of course borrowed two central characters, the girl who is innocent of the world but has a natural desire for love, and the older man who is insecure and hence possessive. But he has abandoned the convent in favour of the simple country upbringing, and the betrothed ward in favour of the girl trapped in marriage. Again there are some smaller debts and verbal echoes. Like Arnolphe, Pinchwife believes men should rule their wives, and so prefers a simple country girl to a smart town woman. The scene in which Margery arouses and allays Pinchwife's jealousy with her innocent prattle (IV.ii) derives from the similar one between Agnes and Arnolphe (II.v.). Here Molière for once indulges in innuendo; Arnolphe wants to know what Horace has taken from Agnes, fearing it is her virginity, when it is in fact her ribbon. Wycherley has a somewhat more salacious version of this incident when Pinchwife torments himself with the idea of Horner's 'beastliness' and Margery describes exactly how he kissed her. Margery's letter to Horner somewhat resembles Agnes's to Horace, but Wycherley borrows the idea of the go-between from *L'École des Maris*, and greatly expands the farcical possibilities of the episode. Broadly, then, Arnolphe, Agnes, and Horace are like Pinchwife, Margery, and Horner. But where Arnolphe is credible and pathetic, Pinchwife is melodramatic and ridiculous. Agnes is a sensible girl, who makes a conventional marriage to Horace, and becomes a less interesting character; Margery is a wild creature, who runs after Horner, and remains attractive. Compared with Horner, Horace is a colourless character; he wants marriage and gets it, but Horner wants women and gets them.

So comparisons with Molière finally emphasise differences between the two dramatists. Molière favours set speeches in couplets, Wycherley racy dialogue in prose. Indeed Molière's plays have an almost mathematical elegance, as they present data, work out possibilities, and demonstrate conclusions. Wycherley's play is equally well constructed but more complicated, and it is hard to say what is concluded. Such differences lead at least one critic to describe Wycherley as a wholly cynical writer;[21] that is a mistake, but elements of cynicism, satire,

---

[21]   John Wilcox, *The Relation of Molière to Restoration Comedy* (Columbia University Press, 1938), pp. 93–4, 103

farce, and bawdy remain to be considered. If they are not simply Wycherley's own, they must have other sources.

Wycherley would surely know Terence's *The Eunuch* (161 BC)[22] – most educated men did, having been introduced to Terence at school – and could have borrowed directly from it. The play is set in Athens, and has two plots. In the first, the lovesick Phaedria and the braggart Thraso woo the courtesan Thais; in the end Phaedria gets the girl, and accepts Thraso as an exploitable hanger-on. In the second, Phaedria's brother Chaerea gets disguised as a eunuch and ravishes the supposed slave-girl Pamphila; but her brother, the countryman Chremes, proves she is a free-born Athenian, so Chaerea can marry her. The first plot is rather like that between Harcourt, Sparkish, and Alithea, and the structural relationship between Phaedria and Chaerea is rather like that between Harcourt and Horner. The second plot is not unlike that between Horner, Margery, and Pinchwife; but Chaerea is only a young scamp, Pamphila only a sex object, and Chremes only an outsider. Above all, it is not Horner's pretence of being a eunuch that enables him to have sex with Margery. *The Eunuch* also features clever servants of both sexes, but Wycherley could have derived Quack and Lucy from other classical or neo-classical sources. Where Wycherley resembles Terence more than Molière is in his cavalier cynicism about aspects of his characters' behaviour which agitate Puritan moralists.

Of course Wycherley need not have gone back to Terence for a sophisticated approach to moral issues. There was also the example of the Jonsonian comedy of humours, with its simplified characterisation, farcical elements, and satirical purpose. Wycherley was especially indebted to *Volpone,* I think, for plot devices and verbal echoes. In one episode, Volpone lusts after Celia, whose fearful husband, Corvino, keeps her locked up. She is virtuous but susceptible, and when she gives Volpone her handkerchief Corvino threatens her with his sword. Volpone feigns a fatal illness, and Corvino is persuaded that he will be made Volpone's heir if he will bring his wife to him. Some parallels are clear: Horner, like Volpone, is a monomaniac who will do anything to get what he wants; Pinchwife, like Corvino, is a ridiculous and deplorable character who deserves to be cuckolded; Margery, like Celia, is not entirely innocent. Pinchwife tells Margery 'be sure you come not within three strides of the window' (IV.ii.200–1), just as

---

[22] In *Terence,* with an English translation by John Sargeaunt (Loeb Library), vol.1, pp. 231–351

Corvino tells Celia he will chalk a line beyond which she must not go 'some two or three yards' from the window (II.v.50–3). Corvino then has the ludicrous idea that he will restrain his wife by making her do everything backwards, leading him to the unintentionally obscene 'no pleasure / That thou shalt know, but backwards'. This is echoed not by Pinchwife but by the more broadly comic cuckold Sir Jaspar Fidget when he warns his wife that Horner 'is coming into you the back way' (IV.iii.132–3). Sir Jaspar and Lady Fidget descend from Jonson's Sir Politick and Lady Would-be, the two gentlemen hoping to impress the state's rulers with their projects, and the two ladies able to embarrass the play's heroes with their attentions.

STAGE HISTORY

The Country Wife was first performed, probably on 12 January 1675, by the King's Company at the Theatre Royal, Drury Lane. This was a new building designed by Sir Christopher Wren, looking in some ways forward to our modern theatres, in others back to the Elizabethan. Like our theatres it was roofed over and needed illumination, but like the Elizabethan it had a large open forestage reaching well into the auditorium. Access to this main acting area was by a pair of doors at either side; a stage direction such as '*Exit* HORNER *at t'other door*' (IV.iii.131) means Horner goes out at the other door on the same side. Behind the forestage was the proscenium arch, and behind that a large recess where scenes were mounted and changed. The recess was dimly lit compared with the rest of the theatre, and the scenes would give only general impressions of the different locales, thus not greatly distracting attention from the actors on the forestage. After the prologue a green curtain was raised to reveal the first scene, but later scene changes were made in view of the audience. Here is an early description of the auditorium:

> The pit is an amphitheatre, filled with benches without backboards, and adorned and covered with green cloth. Men of quality, particularly the younger sort, some ladies of reputation and virtue, and an abundance of damsels that hunt for prey, sit all together in this place, higgledy-piggledy, chatter, toy, play, hear, hear not. Further up, against the wall, under the first gallery, and just opposite to the stage, rises another amphitheatre, which is taken up by persons of the best quality, among whom are generally very few men. The galleries, whereof there are only two rows, are

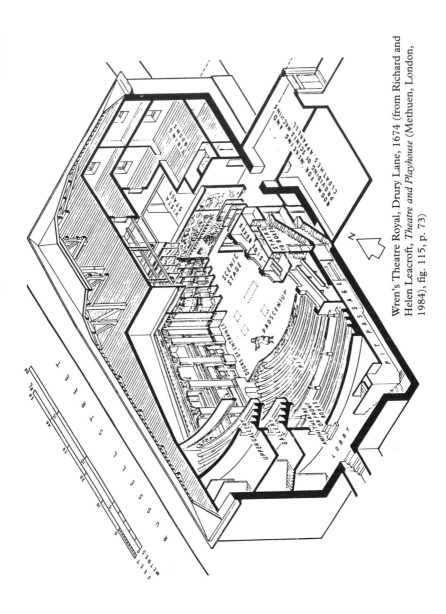

Wren's Theatre Royal, Drury Lane, 1674 (from Richard and Helen Leacroft, *Theatre and Playhouse* (Methuen, London, 1984), fig. 115, p. 73)

filled with none but ordinary people, particularly in the upper one.[23]

The amphitheatre for 'persons of the best quality' was divided into boxes. At the time of the first performance of *The Country Wife* the theatre could have been more dominated by the court than this description suggests, especially if the King favoured it with his presence in the royal box, or the court wits with their comments from the pit. The precise capacity is uncertain, but it can be calculated that the theatre would not seem overcrowded till the audience approached a thousand, and that a performance would remain profitable till it fell below five hundred. So this theatre, though grander than the Elizabethan, remained intimate.

The King's Company was well established and had some experienced players. No doubt they were versatile, but they probably played to their strengths, and Wycherley must have written parts with particular actors and actresses in mind. In any case regular playgoers, recognising the players, would see new roles through memories of old ones – an effect familiar enough today on television and in the cinema. So to understand Wycherley's intentions or the effect *The Country Wife* probably produced, it is vital to know something of the original players.[24] The male leads were Charles Hart as Horner and Edward Kynaston as Harcourt; they had already played against each other as a rake and a romantic in Wycherley's *Love in a Wood*. As Hart was a man of forty-five who had played many major roles in comedy and tragedy, his Horner would have been masterful if potentially dissipated; as Kynaston was young enough to have played women's roles immediately after the Restoration, his Harcourt would have been attractive if potentially effeminate. The comic victims were played by two

[23] M. Misson's *Memoirs and Observations ... Translated by Mr Ozell* (1719), pp. 219-20, quoted in *The London Stage, Part I: 1660–1700*, ed. William van Lennep, introduction by Emmett L. Avery and Arthur H. Scouten (Southern Illinois University Press, 1965), pp. xli–xlii. This introduction and the relevant parts of John Loftis, Richard Southern, Marion Jones, and A.H. Scouten, *The Revels History of Drama in English, Vol. V: 1660–1750* (Methuen, 1976) and *The London Theatre World*, ed. Robert D. Hume (Southern Illinois, 1980), are my main sources of information on the Restoration theatre.

[24] Edward A. Langhans, Philip H. Highfill, Jr., and Kalman A. Burnim, *A Biographical Dictionary of Stage Personnel in London, 1660–1800* (Southern Illinois University Press, 1973-) and correspondence with Professor Langhans are my main sources here and in the notes on the players (pp. 4–5).

elderly actors, Michael Mohun and William Cartwright, and by young Joseph Haines. Mohun was probably best known for playing tragic villains such as Volpone and Iago, and Cartwright for comic characters such as Falstaff and Corbaccio, so Mohun's Pinchwife would probably be alarming as well as funny, and Cartwright's Sir Jaspar a more straightforwardly comic figure. Haines was a song and dance man, already famous for eccentric behaviour both on and off the stage; his buffoonery would perhaps make a highly romantic portrayal of Harcourt and Alithea less likely. The principal women's roles were taken by Mrs Boutell as Mrs Pinchwife, Mrs Knepp as Lady Fidget, and Mrs James as Alithea. Mrs Boutell was

> low of stature, had very agreeable features, a good complexion, but a childish look. Her voice was weak, tho' very mellow; she generally acted the *young innocent lady* whom all the heroes are mad in love with; she was a favourite of the town.[25]

She often appeared in breeches roles, and no doubt looked more attractive than ever when dressed as a boy in III.ii, an effect which Pinchwife foolishly fails to anticipate. But her youth and innocence against Mohun's age and violence could have played for pathos. Certainly her ideas of what she wants and how to get it would remain pathetically vague compared with those of Mrs Knepp's Lady Fidget. Mrs Knepp was more dynamic; Pepys said she was 'the most excellent, mad-humoured thing, and sings the noblest that ever I heard', while her lover, Haines, called her 'that delicate compound of spirit and rump'. One of her earlier comic roles had been Lady Flippant in *Love in a Wood*, another woman whose code of 'honour' conveys appetite for sex, to those who can decode it. Mrs Knepp's various talents would have been put to splendid effect in the great drunken scene at Horner's lodgings. Mrs James had previously played normal but minor characters like Bianca in *Othello*; in the company of Mrs Boutell and Mrs Knepp she is unlikely to have made Alithea the central role demanded by some modern critical interpretations. It seems safe to conclude that the King's Company's performance would have avoided the extremes of pure farce and grim satire.

The evidence that the play 'was an immediate success'[26] is slight. It was acted again during the following season, there

---

[25] Thomas Betterton, *History of the English Stage* (1741), p. 21; this book was apparently compiled from Betterton's notes by William Oldys and Edmund Curll.

[26] *The Country Wife*, ed. David Cook and John Swannell (The Revels Plays, 1975), p. lxiv

were probably revivals during the 1683–4, 1688–9 and 1694–5 seasons, and there could have been others which have not been recorded. Jeremy Collier, in his *Short View of the Immorality and Profaneness of the English Stage* (1698), mentions Wycherley's plays much less often than those of Dryden, Vanbrugh, and others, apparently not because he thought them less offensive, but because they were less popular. But during the first forty years of the eighteenth century *The Country Wife* was a stock piece, 'not tremendously popular but apparently a dependable part of the repertory'; it was especially successful from 1725 to 1742, when there were often rival productions by the two patent companies, employing the best actors and actresses. During the next decade its popularity waned, and in 1753 it was acted for the last time in its original form until the present century.[27]

The offensiveness of the play was immediately remarked on; Wycherley responds to such criticisms in a scene in *The Plain Dealer*, in which the prudish Olivia thinks no modest woman can see *The Country Wife* without blushing, though the sensible Eliza evidently can. Olivia finds 'clandestine obscenity' in the name Horner, and feels that Wycherley has 'quite taken away the reputation of poor *China* itself'. The fop Novel believes all the trouble could have been avoided if only the author had put the play into rhyme, which can make double-meanings pass with the ladies for tender passions. As the scene is an imitation of Molière's *La Critique de L'École des Femmes*, it is not clear what the criticisms of *The Country Wife* really amounted to; it is clear that Wycherley himself thought little of them. But there is some evidence, admittedly tenuous, that the impact of *The Country Wife* began to be modified quite early on. Colley Cibber records that William Mountfort, playing Sparkish some time in the late seventeenth century, gave a 'delightful instance' of his ability to play 'the brisk, vain, rude and lively coxcomb, the false, flashy pretender to wit, and the dupe of his own sufficiency'.[28] This relatively serious conception of the role could imply an attempt to give the Harcourt-Alithea-Sparkish plot greater centrality, and so in a measure moralise the play.

The effect of Collier's moralistic attack on Restoration drama can be felt in Steele's account of a benefit performance for Mrs Bicknell at Drury Lane in 1709.[29] Steele says Mrs Bicknell 'made a very pretty figure, and exactly entered into the nature of

[27]   E.L.Avery, '*The Country Wife* in the Eighteenth Century', *Research Studies*, vol. 10 (1942), 141–72, and 'The Reputation of Wycherley's Comedies as Stage Plays in the Eighteenth Century', ibid., vol. 12 (1942), 132–54

[28]   *An Apology for the Life of Mr Colley Cibber* (1740), ch. 5, p. 77

[29]   *The Tatler*, 16 April 1709

the part' of Mrs Pinchwife. He then feels he must explain the relationship of the Pinchwifes in detail, and defend Wycherley against charges of immorality. We should note Mrs Pinchwife's sad fall from grace, and the satire on Pinchwife:

> The poet on many occasions, where the propriety of the character will admit of it, insinuates that there is no defence against vice, but the contempt of it, and has, in the natural ideas of an untainted innocent, shown the gradual steps to ruin which persons of condition run into, without the help of a good education to form their conduct. The torment of a jealous coxcomb, which arises from his own false maxims, and the aggravation of his pain, by the very words in which he sees her innocence, makes a very pleasant and instructive satire.

But Steele apparently found no sign of satire on Horner, and could only defend Wycherley's portrayal of the rake by a historical argument:

> The character of Horner, and the design of it, is a good representation of the age in which the comedy was written; at which time, love and wenching were the business of life, and the gallant manner of pursuing women was the best recommendation at court. To this only is it to be imputed, that a gentleman of Mr Wycherley's character and sense, condescends to represent the insults done to the honour of the bed, without just reproof.

The feelings that the language of the play was indecent, and its whole tendency immoral, so intensified during the eighteenth century that eventually two revised versions were made. These were John Lee's *The Country Wife* (1765) and Garrick's *The Country Girl* (1766). Lee's version is a two-act entertainment aimed at being 'inoffensively humorous'.[30] Horner, the feigned impotence, and the Fidgets disappear entirely. Dorilant becomes the would-be seducer of Mrs Pinchwife, but finally retires so that she and her husband can try again. Alithea, now unquestionably the heroine, advises Pinchwife to let his wife mingle in society and 'improve that mind, which has hitherto been too un-formed to defend itself from the attacks of its own passions, or from those of others'; that is, she advises the education that Steele said was wanting. She also sensibly prefers Harcourt to Sparkish, and declares that Sparkish does not really love her. Harcourt's disguise as a parson is retained – which would not have pleased Collier – but much of

---

[30] *The Country Wife, A Comedy in Two Acts* (1765), 'Advertisement', title-page, verso

Wycherley's bawdy wit is banished. Garrick's version [31] is essentially worse than Lee's, because although it is a five-act play, it involves a more extensive rewriting of the original. Margery Pinchwife becomes Peggy Thrift, the country girl; Jack Pinchwife becomes Jack Moody, her guardian, who only pretends she is his wife. Old Horner becomes young Belville, Harcourt's nephew, and the main plot concerns Belville and Peggy's successful endeavour to thwart her guardian and get married. Harcourt wins Alithea from Sparkish, but her dowry has doubled with inflation (from £5000 to £10,000), and the settings and allusions have also been updated. It was thought that the comedy now blended 'the witty dialogue of former times' with 'the purity, and happy incidents, of modern dramas'. Not surprisingly, Garrick's version eclipsed Lee's; it reached the New York stage in 1794, and there and in London survived to the end of the nineteenth century and even beyond. But from a modern point of view *The Country Girl* is sentimental and boring, where *The Country Wife* is astringent and provocative.

Wycherley's play returned to the London stage in 1924, when it was presented at the Regent Theatre by the Phoenix Society. The director was Montague Summers, who recalled that 'Mrs Grundy wailed aloud and wrung her mittened hands', as 'the raptured audience rocked with laughter'. [32] But the theatre critics were less enthusiastic, and the play had to wait another ten years for a fully successful professional performance. Meanwhile a production at the Everyman Theatre in 1926 should perhaps be regarded as the last gasp of *The Country Girl*, and one in New York in 1931 was apparently the first performance of *The Country Wife* in America. Then, in 1934 a production by Balliol Holloway at the Ambassadors Theatre had a run of five months and was well received by the critics, and in 1936 one by Tyrone Guthrie at the Old Vic proved beyond doubt that the play had regained its place in the repertoire. In this production Michael Redgrave was Horner, Edith Evans was Lady Fidget, and Ruth Gordon played Mrs Pinchwife with an American accent. It was perhaps not meant to suggest that all American girls were essentially naïve. Miss Gordon had already appeared in an American production of the play, and had to return to appear in another on Broadway, so

---

[31] *The Country Girl,* in *The British Theatre ... With Biographical and Critical Remarks* by Mrs Inchbald (1808), vol. 16. Mrs Inchbald's 'Remarks' (p. 5) are quoted below.

[32] *The Playhouse of Pepys* (Routledge, 1935), pp. 318–19

although the Old Vic Company 'played to capacity every night' the run was limited. The Broadway version was less successful because the cast was comparatively lacking in 'star appeal' and 'gusto'.[33] There was only one London production during the Second World War and the period of austerity afterwards, but since 1955 there have been frequent revivals there, in the provinces, and in America. The most important were perhaps: at the Royal Theatre, Stratford, E.15, directed by Tony Richardson, in 1955; at the Royal Court, directed by George Devine, with Joan Plowright as Mrs Pinchwife, in 1956; at the Chichester Festival, directed by Robert Chetwyn, with Maggie Smith as Mrs Pinchwife and Hugh Paddick as Sparkish, in 1969; and at the National Theatre, directed by Peter Hall, with Albert Finney as Horner, in 1977. The play of course offers an unusually high proportion of good parts, and star actresses and actors have appeared as Mrs Pinchwife, Lady Fidget, Horner, Pinchwife, and Sparkish. The direction the play takes will be determined mainly by the casting, though Hall blames himself for the relative failure of the National Theatre production.[34]

It seems the Chichester Festival production inspired the Warren Beatty film *Shampoo*, but the Old Vic production discouraged professional directors for a decade. Then came five revivals in four years: in 1990, at the Mermaid Theatre, directed by Richard Trethowan, with Fenella Fielding as Lady Fidget; in 1991, a touring production by the Cambridge Theatre Company, directed by Mike Alfreds; in 1992, at Holland Park, directed by Peter Benedict; in 1993, at the Harrogate Festival, directed by Andrew Manley, and at the Swan Theatre, Stratford-upon-Avon, by the Royal Shakespeare Company, directed by Max Stafford-Clark. Also in 1993 there was *Lust*, a musical version by the Heather brothers, at the Theatre Royal, Haymarket. All these were quite widely reviewed, if not always well received. The Mermaid revival suffered from an outbreak of flu among the players, and Ms Fielding stole what was left of the show; the Cambridge from a fit of modishness by the director, and the actors onstage competed for attention with those off. The Holland Park setting encouraged vivacious acting, gorgeous costume, and high fantasy. The three roughly concurrent versions of 1993, however, led to suggestions that the play was especially appropriate at a time when the incompetence and hypocrisy of the nation's governors and moralists had been exposed. The musical could not avoid being called a 'Restoration romp', but the Harrogate revival insisted on contemporary relevance to the extent of omitting the romantic plot.

[33] Tyrone Guthrie, *A Life in the Theatre* (Columbus Books, 1987), p. 165
[34] *Peter Hall's Diaries*, ed. John Goodwin (Hamish Hamilton, 1983), p. 319

The Stratford revival came closest to the text and perhaps the spirit of the play, though it may have been too serious; according to *The Times*, 'a puritan production of a cavalier play'.

THE TEXT

The Country Wife was first published in quarto in 1675 (Q1). By the standards of the time it is a nicely printed book with few errors. The impression that it could have been printed from an author's fair copy is supported by the unusually detailed stage directions.[35] The first quarto was reprinted in 1683 (Q2), and the second in 1688 (Q3) and 1695 (Q4). These reprints correct some errors but make quite a lot more. Q4 was very inaccurately reprinted in the same year (Q5).[36] Perhaps because Q4 tried to regularise the spelling and punctuation it was also the copy text for the octavo edition of Wycherley's *Works* in 1713 (O). This was the last edition in the author's lifetime. There is no evidence that he ever revised the text; if he had, presumably he would have corrected some obvious errors which survived the printing process.[37]

The copy text for this edition is the Cambridge University Library copy of Q1 (in the Brett-Smith collection), collated with the Readex microprint of the Library of Congress copy, the University Microfilms (Ann Arbor) microfilm of the Huntington Library copy, and the Scolar Press facsimile of the British Library copy. I have also examined the Cambridge University Library copies of Q2–5 and O. Departures from Q1 involving changes of wording have been recorded in the footnotes, where readings from Q2–5 and O are sometimes quoted in support. Speech prefixes have been expanded, and for the sake of clarity MR has been dropped before Pinchwife's name but MRS has been retained before his wife's. In the stage directions *Mistress*

[35] Cook and Swannell (note 25), p. lxxi. Directions which indicate more than stage business include 'ALITHEA *walks carelessly to and fro*' (III.ii.275), 'MRS PINCHWIFE *alone leaning on her elbow*' (IV.iv.1) and 'PINCHWIFE *stands doggedly, with his hat over his eyes*' (V.iv.297).

[36] Q5 has the running-title '*The Country Wife*', where Q1–4 and O have '*The Country-Wife*'. Q4 and Q5 were carefully distinguished by Robert N.E. Megaw, 'Notes on Restoration Plays (1)', *Studies in Bibliography*, vol. 3 (1951–2), 252–3, except that, as T.H. Fujimura notes in his edition of *The Country Wife* (Regents Restoration Drama Series, 1965), p. ix, Q4 is based on Q2 not Q3.

[37] See for examples IV.iii.205–7 note and V.iv.385, 388 note.

and *Mrs.* have been regularised to MRS (for Mrs Pinchwife) and *Mrs* for the other ladies, while in the text, Mr. and Mrs. have been expanded to Master and Mistress. It is hoped that these procedures will not be thought sexist. Additions to the text, mostly stage directions, are given in square brackets. Directions for asides are placed before the speeches to which they refer. Spelling and punctuation are modernised in line with New Mermaid policy. Modernising the punctuation presents both opportunities and problems; where speeches have a rhetorical structure it can often be clarified, but Q1 often employs dashes to show theatrical pauses of varying lengths. These dashes have sometimes been replaced by the punctuation we would expect from the grammar, and have sometimes been retained, to show transitions from asides to dialogue, parenthetical remarks, and unfinished sentences. I believe the text is suitable for both reading and acting, though a scholarly director bent on authenticity would doubtless make a fresh start with Q1.

FURTHER READING

As the introduction will have suggested, I think the student would do well to read sources or analogues, in translation where necessary: Terence's *The Eunuch*, Jonson's *Volpone*, Molière's *L'École des Maris* and *L'École des Femmes*. I would also recommend reading Wycherley's earlier plays and *The Plain Dealer* (ed. James L. Smith, New Mermaid, 1979), Etherege's *The Man of Mode* (ed. John Barnard, New Mermaid, 1979), and Congreve's *The Way of the World* (ed. Brian Gibbons, New Mermaid, 1971). Students who feel obliged to rely on secondary sources are urged to read several, and to consider the degree to which different interpretations can be reconciled.

Editions

The Complete Plays of William Wycherley, ed. Gerald Weales (New York University Press, 1967). Old spelling.
The Plays of William Wycherley, ed. Arthur Friedman (Oxford, 1979). Old spelling.
The Plays of William Wycherley, ed. Peter Holland (Cambridge, 1981). Modernised text; available in paperback.

Books

Birdsall, Virginia Ogden, *Wild Civility: The English Comic Spirit on the Restoration Stage* (Indiana University Press, 1970). Three chapters on Wycherley.
Chadwick, W.R., *The Four Plays of William Wycherley* (Mouton, 1975). Clear and comprehensive.
Harwood, John T., *Critics, Values, and Restoration Comedy* (Southern Illinois University Press, 1982). On *The Country Wife* and its critics, pp. 98–114.
Holland, Norman N., *The First Modern Comedies* (Harvard, 1959). Four chapters on Wycherley.
McCarthy, B. Eugene, *William Wycherley: A Biography* (Ohio University Press, 1979)
Milhous, Judith, and Robert D. Hume, *Producible Interpretation* (Southern Illinois University Press, 1985). Excellent chapter on *The Country Wife* and its interpreters.
Powell, Jocelyn, *Restoration Theatre Production* (Routledge, 1984). Excellent chapter on *The Country Wife*.
Rogers, K.M., *William Wycherley* (Twayne's English Authors, 1972). An 'overview' or survey; dated on the biographical side.

Thompson, James, *Language in Wycherley's Plays* (University of Alabama Press, 1984). Chapter on 'Figurative Language in *The Country Wife*'.

Weber, Harold, *The Restoration Rake-Hero* (University of Wisconsin Press, 1986). On Horner, pp. 53–69.

Zimbardo, Rose A., *Wycherley's Drama: A Link in the Development of English Satire* (Yale, 1965)

Essays

Burke, Helen, 'Wycherley's "Tendentious Joke": The Discourse of Alterity in *The Country Wife*', *The Eighteenth Century: Theory and Interpretation*, vol. 29 (1988), 227–41. A feminist view.

Cohen, Derek, 'The Revenger's Comedy: A Reading of *The Country Wife*', *Durham University Journal*, vol. 76 (1983), 31–6

Craik, T.W., 'Some Aspects of Satire in Wycherley's Plays', *English Studies*, vol. 41 (1960), 168–79

Duncan, Douglas, 'Mythic Parody in *The Country Wife*', *Essays in Criticism*, vol. 31 (1981), 299–312. Interesting, but tough.

Edgley, R., 'The Object of Literary Criticism', *Essays in Criticism*, vol. 14 (1964), 221–36. On *The Country Wife*, 231–6.

Kaufman, Anthony, 'The Shadow of the Burlador: Don Juan on the Continent and in England,' *Comedy from Shakespeare to Sheridan*, ed. A.R. Braunmuller and J.C. Bulman (Associated University Presses) (1986), pp. 229–54. Horner and other Don Juans.

Love, Harold, 'The Theatrical Geography of *The Country Wife*', *Southern Review* (Adelaide), vol. 16 (1983), 404–15

Malekin, Peter, 'Wycherley's Dramatic Skills and the Interpretation of *The Country Wife*', *Durham University Journal*, vol. 61 (1969), 32–40

Neill, Michael, 'Horned Beasts and China Oranges: Reading the Signs in *The Country Wife*', *Eighteenth Century Life*, vol. 12 (1988), 3–17

Righter, Anne, 'William Wycherley', *Restoration Theatre* (Stratford-upon-Avon Studies, vol. 6; Arnold 1965), pp. 70–91

Thompson, Peggy, 'The Limits of Parody in *The Country Wife*', *Studies in Philology*, vol 89 (1992), 100-14. On 'Wycherley's ambivalent approach to the myth of a sexual fall'.

Vieth, David M., 'Wycherley's *The Country Wife:* An Anatomy of Masculinity', *Papers on Language and Literature*, vol. 2 (1966), 335–50

Reference

Hume, Robert D., 'William Wycherley: Text, Life, Interpretation', *Modern Philology*, vol. 78 (1981), 399–415. Evaluative.

McCarthy, B. Eugene, *William Wycherley: A Reference Guide* (G.K. Hall, 1985). Comprehensive; annotated.

Theatre Record, vols. 10 (1990), 1672–4; 11 (1991), 1505–6; 12 (1992), 873; 13 (1993), 930–7, 827–31. Collected reviews of the productions of those years.

ABBREVIATIONS

Cook and Swannell	David Cook and John Swannell (eds.), *The Country Wife* (The Revels Plays, 1975)
ed.	editor; in the textual notes, indicates a reading not found in Q1–5 and O.
Etherege	References to *The Man of Mode* are to John Barnard's New Mermaid edition.
Farmer and Henley	J.S. Farmer and W.E. Henley, *A Dictionary of Slang* (1890–1904; Wordsworth Editions, 1987)
Friedman	Arthur Friedman (ed.), *The Plays of William Wycherley* (Oxford, 1979). References to Wycherley's Plays other than *The Country Wife* are to this edition.
Holland	Peter Holland (ed.), *The Plays of William Wycherley* (Cambridge, 1981)
Hunt	John Dixon Hunt (ed.), *The Country Wife* (New Mermaid, 1973)
Jonson	References to *Volpone* and *The Alchemist* are to *The Complete Plays of Ben Jonson*, ed. G.A. Wilkes (Oxford, 1982) vol. III.
Markley	Robert Markley, *Two-Edg'd Weapons: Style and Ideology in the Comedies of Etherege, Wycherley and Congreve* (Oxford, 1988)
O	The octavo edition of Wycherley's *Works* (1713)
OED	*Oxford English Dictionary*, 2nd. ed. (1989)
Partridge	Eric Partridge, *A Dictionary of Historical Slang*, abridged by Jacqueline Simpson (Penguin, 1972)
Q1, 2, 3, 4, 5	The quarto editions of *The Country Wife* (1675, 1683, 1688, 1695); see section on 'The Text', pp. xxxvi–xxxvii.
sd	stage direction
Shakespeare	References to the plays are to *The Complete Works*, ed. Stanley Wells and Gary Taylor (Oxford, 1986).
sp	speech prefix; i.e., the name of a character prefixed to a speech
Weales	Gerald Weales (ed.), *The Complete Plays of William Wycherley* (New York University Press, 1967)

THE

Country - Wife,

A

COMEDY,

Acted at the

THEATRE ROYAL.

Written by Mr. *Wycherley.*

*Indignor quicquam reprehendi, non quia crassè
Compositum illepidéve putetur, sed quia nuper:
Nec veniam Antiquis, sed honorem & præmia posci.*
Horat.

LONDON,
Printed for *Thomas Dring*, at the *Harrow*, at the
Corner of *Chancery-Lane* in *Fleet-street.* 1675.

Title-page from the copy in Cambridge University Library, in the H.F.B. Brett-Smith collection, reproduced by permission of the Syndics of Cambridge University Library

Indignior some copies of Q1 (*Indignor* other copies, Q2–5, O). *Indignor* is correct.

Motto Horace, *Epistles* 2.1.76–8. Dryden quoted the first two lines in his *Of Dramatick Poesie* (1668) and mentioned Terence's *The Eunuch* as a play by an ancient writer which is not faultless. As *The Eunuch* is one of his sources, Wycherley could be implying specifically that it deserved only indulgence (*veniam*), while his own play deserved honour and rewards (*honorem & praemia*); or he could be thinking generally of ancient writers. Pope's version in the *Imitations of Horace* is:

> I lose my patience, and I own it too,
> When works are censured, not as bad, but new;
> While if our elders break all reason's laws,
> These fools demand not pardon, but applause.   (*Epistle* 2.1.115–18)

THE PERSONS

MR HORNER

MR HARCOURT

MR DORILANT

MR PINCHWIFE

MR SPARKISH

SIR JASPAR FIDGET

MRS MARGERY PINCHWIFE

MRS ALITHEA

MY LADY FIDGET

MRS DAINTY FIDGET

MRS SQUEAMISH

OLD LADY SQUEAMISH

WAITERS, SERVANTS, AND ATTENDANTS

A BOY

A QUACK

LUCY, *Alithea's Maid*

Mr Hart

Mr Kynaston

Mr Lydall

Mr Mohun

Mr Haines

Mr Cartwright

Mrs Boutell

Mrs James

Mrs Knepp

Mrs Corbet

Mrs Wyatt

Mrs Rutter

Mr Shatterell

Mrs Corey

The Scene: *London*

The Persons This cast list is illogically placed after the prologue in Q1 and most modern editions. It omits Clasp, a bookseller, mentioned at III.ii.159, and a parson mentioned in the stage direction at V.iv.227.

HORNER: maker of cuckolds (see I.i.83, note); the word is used in this sense by John Fletcher in *The Elder Brother* (1637) IV.iv. To Olivia in *The Plain Dealer* 'the very name' suggests 'the image of a goat, a town-bull, or a satyr' (II.i.412–15), that is, a lecherous creature. Also associated with the Devil, traditionally represented as horned, and a not uncommon English surname which occurs in the rhyme 'Little Jack Horner'. But Horner's Christian name is Harry (I.i.286), again associated with both womanisers (see V.iv.177, note) and the Devil ('Old Harry').

HARCOURT suggests an English gentleman; perhaps derived from place names in Shropshire. His Christian name is Frank (II.i.187 and elsewhere) and it may be significant that his rival Sparkish falsely claims frankness as a virtue.

DORILANT suggests *jeunesse dorée*; perhaps derived from Dorante, a common name for such characters in contemporary French drama, and a source for the name Dorimant, the rake-hero of *The Man of Mode*. Dorilant's Christian name is Dick (I.i.290 and II.i.187).

PINCHWIFE: one who restricts his wife's freedom; she expects him to 'pinch' her (IV.iii.289). His Christian name is Jack (I.i.359).

SPARKISH: a bit of a 'spark', a young man who affects smartness in dress and manners. The only major character whose Christian name is not given.

JASPAR FIDGET: name with various associations. Jaspar derives from Caspar, 'keeper of the treasure', the Magus traditionally supposed to represent the black races; its association with villains belongs to Victorian melodrama. Fidget suggests a busybody; in *Love in a Wood* 'a politic wit' is defined as 'a fidgeting, busy, dogmatical, hot-headed fop' (II.i.261), and Sir Jaspar's 'business' is political rather than commercial (see I.i.115–16 and notes, and introduction, p. xvi).

MARGERY perhaps already suggested a sluttish country girl, like Margery Daw; see Iona and Peter Opie, *Oxford Dictionary of Nursery Rhymes* (1977) p. 298. In *The Merchant of Venice* Old Gobbo, a rustic, has a wife called Margery (II.ii.84–6).

ALITHEA: derived from the Greek word for 'truth'; a fashionable name in the seventeenth century

DAINTY: fastidious (*OED a.*5); not a true Christian name

SQUEAMISH: prudish (*OED* 7). Mrs Squeamish's Christian name may be Bridget (IV.iii.178 and note).

QUACK: boastful pretender to knowledge, especially in medicine

LUCY: derived from the Latin word for 'light'

Players

Hart, Charles (*c.* 1630–83), a sharer in the King's Company and a leading actor, famous for heroic roles, including Almanzor in Dryden's *Conquest of Granada* and several Shakespearean tragic figures. His comic roles had included Mosca in *Volpone* and Ranger in *Love in a Wood,* and he had been the lover of both Nell Gwyn and Lady Castlemaine.

Kynaston, Edward (1643–1712), a leading actor, was originally famous for women's roles, later for romantic heroes, including Valentine in *Love in a Wood* .

Lydall or Lidell, Edward (fl. 1655–77), a regular actor who did not often take major roles

Mohun, Michael (1616?–84), a sharer in the King's Company and a leading actor, whose roles had included villains and rogues: Cassius in *Julius Caesar,* Iago, Volpone, Face in *The Alchemist,* and Dapperwit in *Love in a Wood*

Haines, Joseph (1648?–1701), a young comedian, already famous for eccentricity both on and off the stage. See Kenneth M. Cameron, 'Jo Haynes, Infamis', *Theatre Notebook* vol. 24 (1969–70), 56–67.

Cartwright, William (*c.* 1604–86), a sharer in the King's Company and a leading comedian, whose roles had included Falstaff, Corbaccio in *Volpone,* and Sir Epicure Mammon in *The Alchemist*

Boutell or Bowtell, Mrs Barnaby, née Elizabeth Davenport (*c.* 1649–1715), a versatile and popular actress who had played major roles in heroic plays and tragedies and breeches roles in comedies and farces. She was small and pretty and 'generally acted the *young innocent lady* whom all the heroes are mad in love with; she was a favourite of the town' (Introduction, note 25). See Judith Milhous, 'Elizabeth Bowtell and Elizabeth Davenport: Some Problems Solved', *Theatre Notebook* vol. 39 (1985), 124–34.

James, Elizabeth (fl. 1669–1703?), took mainly minor roles, including Isabel in *Love in a Wood.*

Knepp, Mrs Christopher, née Elizabeth Carpenter (fl. 1659–81), famous as both actress and singer; her comic roles had included Lady Flippant in *Love in a Wood.* See Robert Latham (ed.), *The Diary of Samuel Pepys,* vol. 10 (Bell and Hyman, 1983), pp. 215–16.

Corbet, Mary (fl. 1670?–82?), took mainly minor roles.

Wyatt, Mrs, otherwise unknown

Rutter, Margaret (fl. 1661–*c.* 1680), took mainly minor roles, including Emilia in *Othello* and Mrs Crossbite in *Love in a Wood,* 'an old cheating jilt, and bawd to her daughter'.

Shatterell, Robert (born *c.* 1615?), a senior member of the King's Company, played mainly character parts such as Voltore in *Volpone* and Poins in *Henry IV, Part I.*

Corey, Mrs John, née Katherine Mitchell (born *c.* 1635), one of the first English actresses and women members of the King's Company, who often played comic servants and bawds. Her roles had included Doll Common in *The Alchemist,* Lady Would-be in *Volpone,* and Mrs Joyner in *Love in a Wood.*

PROLOGUE

Spoken by Mr Hart

Poets, like cudgelled bullies, never do
At first or second blow submit to you;
But will provoke you still and ne'er have done,
Till you are weary first with laying on.
The late so baffled scribbler of this day,   5
Though he stands trembling, bids me boldly say,
What we before most plays are used to do,
For poets out of fear first draw on you;
In a fierce prologue the still pit defy,
And, ere you speak, like Castril give the lie.   10
But though our Bayeses' battles oft I've fought,
And with bruised knuckles their dear conquests bought;
Nay, never yet feared odds upon the stage,
In prologue dare not hector with the age,
But would take quarter from your saving hands,   15
Though Bayes within all yielding countermands,
Says you confederate wits no quarter give,
Therefore his play shan't ask your leave to live.
Well, let the vain rash fop, by huffing so,
Think to obtain the better terms of you;   20
But we, the actors, humbly will submit,
Now, and at any time, to a full pit;
Nay, often we anticipate your rage,
And murder poets for you on our stage.
We set no guards upon our tiring-room,   25
But when with flying colours there you come,
We patiently, you see, give up to you
Our poets, virgins, nay, our matrons too.

1 *bullies* London street ruffians   4 *laying on* inflicting blows
5 *late so baffled scribbler* Wycherley himself; either because *The Gentleman Dancing-Master* (1672) had not succeeded on the stage, or because *The Plain Dealer*, which may have already been written, had not yet been staged
10 *Castril* the 'angry boy' in Jonson's *The Alchemist,* who accuses Subtle of lying almost before he speaks (IV.ii.19)
11 *our Bayeses' battles* our poets' battles generally, though the speaker had played heroic parts in Dryden's tragedies, and the name Bayes was associated especially with Dryden. See l.16 below.
14 *hector with the age* attack contemporary taste
16 *Bayes within* Wycherley behind the scenes
17 *confederate* conspiring (to damn the play)   19 *huffing* blustering
25 *tiring-room* dressing room   27–8 See II.i.360–2 and note.

THE COUNTRY WIFE

Act I, Scene i

Enter HORNER, *and* QUACK *following him at a distance*

HORNER (*Aside*)
> A quack is as fit for a pimp as a midwife for a bawd;
> they are still but in their way both helpers of nature. –
> Well, my dear doctor, hast thou done what I desired?

QUACK
> I have undone you for ever with the women, and
> reported you throughout the whole town as bad as an   5
> eunuch, with as much trouble as if I had made you one
> in earnest.

HORNER
> But have you told all the midwives you know, the orange
> wenches at the playhouses, the city husbands, and old
> fumbling keepers of this end of the town? For they'll be   10
> the readiest to report it.

QUACK
> I have told all the chamber-maids, waiting-women, tire-
> women and old women of my acquaintance; nay, and
> whispered it as a secret to 'em, and to the whisperers of
> Whitehall. So that you need not doubt 'twill spread,   15
> and you will be as odious to the handsome young
> women as –

HORNER
> As the smallpox. Well –

---

2 *still* always

8–9 *orange wenches* sellers of oranges and other refreshments

9 *city husbands* men who will be glad to hear of Horner's impotence
and, according to a convention of Restoration comedy, easily cuckolded.
There was hostility between citizens and courtiers, the citizens accusing
the courtiers of immorality, and the courtiers accusing the citizens of
hypocrisy.

9–10 *old fumbling keepers of this end of the town* incompetent keepers of
mistresses living in the fashionable part of the town. From I.i.301–16 we
gather that Horner lives in Russell Street, Covent Garden.

12–13 *tire-women* ladies' maids

15 *Whitehall* the public rooms at the King's palace, where gossip flourished

QUACK

And to the married women of this end of the town as –

HORNER

As the great ones; nay, as their own husbands.   20

QUACK

And to the city dames as Aniseed Robin of filthy and
contemptible memory;   and they will frighten their
children with your name, especially their females.

HORNER

And cry, 'Horner's coming to carry you away!'   I am
only afraid 'twill not be believed.   You told 'em 'twas by   25
an English-French disaster, and an English-French
surgeon, who has given me at once not only a cure but
an antidote for the future against that damned malady,
and that worse distemper, love, and all other women's
evils?   30

QUACK

Your late journey into France has made it the more
credible, and your being here a fortnight before you
appeared in public looks as if you apprehended the
shame;   which I wonder you do not.   Well, I have been
hired by young gallants to belie 'em t'other way, but you   35
are the first would be thought a man unfit for women.

HORNER

Dear Master Doctor, let vain rogues be contented only
to be thought abler men than they are, generally 'tis all
the pleasure they have;   but mine lies another way.

QUACK

You take, methinks, a very preposterous way to it, and as   40

---

20   *the great ones* syphilis;   the great pox, or syphilis, as opposed to the
small ones, or smallpox.   Pox is the plural of pock.

21   *Aniseed Robin*   well-known hermaphrodite who sold aniseed water (a
carminative) on the London streets;   said to have been both a father and
a mother (Charles Cotton, *Poems,* ed. John Beresford, p. 288)

26–7   *English-French disaster, and an English-French surgeon*   Could mean pox,
caught with the aid of an English bawd, and operated on by a surgeon
specialising in venereal disease;   everything to do with pox could be
loosely associated with France.   This interpretation is supported by
Horner's remark at V.iv.55.   But as I.i. emphasises that Horner has been
in France, Lady Fidget thinks the disaster and/or operation has taken
place there;   see II.i.561–2.

27–8   *not only a cure but an antidote* because the story is that the surgeon has
made him a eunuch

ridiculous as if we operators in physic should put forth
bills to disparage our medicaments, with hopes to gain
customers.

HORNER

Doctor, there are quacks in love, as well as physic, who
get but the fewer and worse patients for their boasting.   45
A good name is seldom got by giving it oneself, and
women no more than honour are compassed by
bragging. Come, come, doctor, the wisest lawyer never
discovers the merits of his cause till the trial. The
wealthiest man conceals his riches, and the cunning   50
gamester his play. Shy husbands and keepers, like old
rooks, are not to be cheated but by a new unpractised
trick. False friendship will pass now no more than false
dice upon 'em; no, not in the city.

Enter BOY

BOY

There are two ladies and a gentleman coming up.   55

[*Exit* BOY]

HORNER

A pox! Some unbelieving sisters of my former acquaintance who, I am afraid, expect their sense should be
satisfied of the falsity of the report.

Enter SIR JASPAR, LADY FIDGET *and Mrs* DAINTY FIDGET

No; this formal fool and women!

QUACK

His wife and sister.   60

SIR JASPER

My coach breaking just now before your door sir, I look

47 *compassed* won
49 *discovers* reveals
52 *rooks* tricksters. See also I.i.265.
53–4 *pass upon* impose upon
56 *sisters* disguised prostitutes (Farmer and Henley)
59 *formal* ceremonious
61–83 Horner mocks Sir Jaspar's repetition of 'sir'. I have followed Q1 in
      omitting commas before 'sir' in Sir Jaspar's speeches at ll. 61–5 and 71,
      and in inserting them before it in Horner's speeches; as Peter Malekin
      says, Q1 hints at how the scene was or should be played ('Wycherley's
      Dramatic Skills and the Interpretation of *The Country Wife*', *Durham
      University Journal*, vol. 61 (1969), 32–40). But elsewhere the omission
      of commas before 'sir' does not seem significant, and I have followed
      modern practice in inserting them.

upon as an occasional reprimand to me sir, for not
kissing your hands sir, since your coming out of France
sir; and so my disaster sir, has been my good fortune sir;
and this is my wife, and sister sir.   65
HORNER
What then, sir?
SIR JASPER
My lady, and sister, sir. – Wife, this is Master Horner.
LADY FIDGET
Master Horner, husband!
SIR JASPAR
My lady, my Lady Fidget, sir.
HORNER
So, sir.   70
SIR JASPAR
Won't you be acquainted with her sir? (*Aside*) So, the
report is true, I find, by his coldness or aversion to the
sex; but I'll play the wag with him. – Pray salute my
wife, my lady, sir.
HORNER
I will kiss no man's wife, sir, for him, sir; I have taken   75
my eternal leave, sir, of the sex already, sir.
SIR JASPAR (*Aside*)
Ha, ha, ha! I'll plague him yet. – Not know my wife,
sir?
HORNER
I do know your wife, sir, she's a woman, sir, and
consequently a monster, sir, a greater monster than a   80
husband, sir.
SIR JASPAR
A husband! How, sir?
HORNER (*Makes horns*)
So, sir. But I make no more cuckolds, sir.
SIR JASPAR
Ha, ha, ha! Mercury, Mercury!

62   *occasional* timely
73   *play the wag with him* have a joke at his expense. See also IV.iii.148–51.
83   sd *horns* sign of a cuckold; *cuckolds* husbands of adulterous wives. For
     obvious reasons adulterers were known as cuckoos, and their victims
     came to be called cuckolds, but it is not clear why cuckolds were
     supposed to have horns.
84   *Mercury* god associated with wit. Also, substance used to treat venereal
     disease; but perhaps Horner making horns reminds Sir Jaspar of
     representations of Mercury with a winged hat.

LADY FIDGET

Pray, Sir Jaspar, let us be gone from this rude fellow.   85

DAINTY

Who, by his breeding, would think he had ever been in
France?

LADY FIDGET

Foh! he's but too much a French fellow, such as hate
women of quality and virtue for their love to their
husbands, Sir Jaspar. A woman is hated by 'em as much   90
for loving her husband as for loving their money. But
pray let's be gone.

HORNER

You do well, madam, for I have nothing that you came
for. I have brought over not so much as a bawdy
picture, new postures, nor the second part of the *École*   95
des Filles, nor –

QUACK (*Apart* to HORNER)

Hold for shame sir! What d'ye mean? You'll ruin
yourself for ever with the sex –

SIR JASPAR

Ha, ha, ha! He hates women perfectly, I find.

DAINTY

What pity 'tis he should.   100

LADY FIDGET

Ay, he's a base rude fellow for't; but affectation makes
not a woman more odious to them than virtue.

HORNER

Because your virtue is your greatest affectation, madam.

LADY FIDGET

How, you saucy fellow! Would you wrong my honour?

HORNER

If I could.   105

LADY FIDGET

How d'ye mean, sir?

SIR JASPAR

Ha, ha, ha! No, he can't wrong your ladyship's honour,
upon my honour! He, poor man – hark you in your ear
– a mere eunuch.

---

88 *French fellow* fop
95 *postures* erotic engravings used to illustrate pornographic books
95–6 *École des Filles* (1668), 'the most bawdy, lewd book that ever I saw ... so
      that I was ashamed of reading it' (Pepys, *Diary,* 16 January 1668)
104 *How* what

LADY FIDGET

O filthy French beast! foh, foh! Why do we stay? Let's 110
be gone. I can't endure the sight of him.

SIR JASPAR

Stay but till the chairs come. They'll be here presently.

LADY FIDGET

No, no.

SIR JASPAR

Nor can I stay longer. 'Tis – let me see – a quarter and a
half quarter of a minute past eleven. The Council will 115
be sat, I must away. Business must be preferred always
before love and ceremony with the wise, Master Horner.

HORNER

And the impotent, Sir Jaspar.

SIR JASPAR

Ay, ay, the impotent, Master Horner, ha, ha, ha!

LADY FIDGET

What, leave us with a filthy man alone in his lodgings?   120

SIR JASPAR

He's an innocent man now, you know. Pray stay, I'll
hasten the chairs to you. Master Horner, your servant;
I should be glad to see you at my house. Pray come and
dine with me, and play at cards with my wife after
dinner; you are fit for women at that game yet, ha, ha! 125
(*Aside*) 'Tis as much a husband's prudence to provide
innocent diversion for a wife as to hinder her unlawful
pleasures; and he had better employ her, than let her
employ herself. – Farewell.

Exit SIR JASPAR

HORNER

Your servant, Sir Jaspar.   130

LADY FIDGET

I will not stay with him, foh!

---

112 *chairs* sedan chairs
       presently at once
115 *Council* Privy Council
116 *Business* at court, not in the City. See Introduction, p. xiv
128 *employ* keep busy

HORNER

Nay, madam, I beseech you stay, if it be but to see I can
be as civil to ladies yet as they would desire.

LADY FIDGET

No, no, foh! You cannot be civil to ladies.

DAINTY

You as civil as ladies would desire?   135

LADY FIDGET

No, no, no! foh, foh, foh!

Exeunt LADY FIDGET *and* DAINTY

QUACK

Now I think, I, or you yourself rather, have done your
business with the women.

HORNER

Thou art an ass. Don't you see already, upon the report
and my carriage, this grave man of business leaves his 140
wife in my lodgings, invites me to his house and wife,
who before would not be acquainted with me out of
jealousy?

QUACK

Nay, by this means you may be the more acquainted
with the husbands, but the less with the wives.   145

HORNER

Let me alone; if I can but abuse the husbands, I'll soon
disabuse the wives. Stay; I'll reckon you up the
advantages I am like to have by my stratagem. First, I
shall be rid of all my old acquaintances, the most
insatiable sorts of duns, that invade our lodgings in a 150
morning. And next to the pleasure of making a new
mistress is that of being rid of an old one, and of all old

133–5 *civil* probably with a sexual connotation: 'You are both very civil
gentlemen – and my wife, there, is a very civil gentlewoman; therefore I
don't doubt but many civil things have passed between you' (Vanbrugh,
The Provoked Wife, ed. James L. Smith, V.ii.83–5).

137–8 *done your business* ruined you

140 *carriage* conduct

146 *abuse* deceive. The word probably has modern sense at I.i.242.

150 *duns* importunate creditors; apparently referring to I.i.56–7

151 *next* Q2–5, O (next, Q1). The Q1 comma suggests Horner is
counting his advantages, 'first' one 'and next' another. But he actually
says 'next to' the pleasure of taking a mistress is that of discarding one;
so I have discarded the comma. Markley suggests that Horner, unable
to count many advantages, changes his mind about what he is saying.

debts; love, when it comes to be so, is paid the most unwillingly.

QUACK

Well, you may be so rid of your old acquaintances, but 155
how will you get any new ones?

HORNER

Doctor, thou wilt never make a good chemist, thou art so incredulous and impatient. Ask but all the young fellows of the town, if they do not lose more time, like huntsmen, in starting the game, than in running it 160 down. One knows not where to find 'em who will, or will not. Women of quality are so civil, you can hardly distinguish love from good breeding, and a man is often mistaken. But now I can be sure she that shows an aversion to me loves the sport; as those women that are 165 gone, whom I warrant to be right. And then the next thing is, your women of honour, as you call 'em, are only chary of their reputations, not their persons, and 'tis scandal they would avoid, not men. Now may I have, by the reputation of an eunuch, the privileges of 170 one; and be seen in a lady's chamber in a morning as early as her husband; kiss virgins before their parents or lovers; and may be, in short, the *passe-partout* of the town. Now doctor?

QUACK

Nay, now you shall be the doctor. And your process is 175
so new that we do not know but it may succeed.

HORNER

Not so new neither. *Probatum est,* doctor.

QUACK

Well, I wish you luck and many patients whilst I go to mine.

Exit QUACK

---

157 *chemist* alchemist. In Jonson's *The Alchemist* the clients' incredulity and impatience are supposed to harm the alchemical process.

158–64 The problem is to distinguish the game from other creatures.

166 *right* ready for the sport, 'game'. See *The Gentleman Dancing-Master* III.i.530, and the note in Friedman, p. 189.

173 *passe-partout* person having leave to go anywhere

175 *doctor* alchemist
     process alchemical experiment

177 *probatum est* proved or tested; phrase written on prescriptions. Horner apparently means that in the sex game nothing is wholly new. Wycherley possibly hints at his own borrowing from Terence; see Introduction, p. xxvi.

Enter HARCOURT *and* DORILANT *to* HORNER

HARCOURT

Come, your appearance at the play yesterday has, I   180
hope, hardened you for the future against the women's
contempt and the men's raillery, and now you'll abroad
as you were wont.

HORNER

Did I not bear it bravely?

DORILANT

With a most theatrical impudence! Nay, more than the   185
orange-wenches show there, or a drunken vizard-mask,
or a great-bellied actress. Nay, or the most impudent of
creatures, an ill poet. Or, what is yet more impudent, a
second-hand critic.

HORNER

But what say the ladies? Have they no pity?   190

HARCOURT

What ladies? The vizard-masks, you know, never pity a
man when all's gone, though in their service.

DORILANT

And for the women in the boxes, you'd never pity them
when 'twas in your power.

HARCOURT

They say 'tis pity, but all that deal with common women   195
should be served so.

DORILANT

Nay, I dare swear, they won't admit you to play at cards
with them, go to plays with 'em, or do the little duties
which other shadows of men are wont to do for 'em.

HORNER

Who do you call shadows of men?   200

DORILANT

Half-men.

HORNER

What, boys?

DORILANT

Ay, your old boys, old *beaux garçons*, who like super-

---

186 *vizard-mask* (here) prostitute. Just after the Restoration masks had been
       fashionable wear, but by this time they had become professional gear.
192 *all* sexual potency or money
193 *women in the boxes* 'persons of the best quality, among whom are
       generally very few men' occupied the boxes. See Introduction, p. xxix.
203 *beaux garçons* fops

annuated stallions are suffered to run, feed, and whinny
with the mares as long as they live, though they can do 205
nothing else.

HORNER

Well, a pox on love and wenching! Women serve but to
keep a man from better company. Though I can't enjoy
them, I shall you the more.   Good fellowship and
friendship are lasting, rational, and manly pleasures.   210

HARCOURT

For all that, give me some of those pleasures you call
effeminate too. They help to relish one another.

HORNER

They disturb one another.

HARCOURT

No, mistresses are like books; if you pore upon them
too much they doze you and make you unfit for com- 215
pany, but if used discreetly you are the fitter for
conversation by 'em.

DORILANT

A mistress should be like a little country retreat near the
town; not to dwell in constantly, but only for a night
and away, to taste the town the better when a man 220
returns.

HORNER

I tell you, 'tis as hard to be a good fellow, a good friend,
and a lover of women, as 'tis to be a good fellow, a good
friend, and a lover of money. You cannot follow both,
then choose your side: wine gives you liberty, love takes **225**
it away.

DORILANT

Gad, he's in the right on't.

HORNER

Wine gives you joy; love, grief and tortures, besides the
surgeon's. Wine makes us witty; love, only sots. Wine

---

215 *doze* make drowsy or dull
217 *conversation* intercourse; a *double entendre*. See also II.i.560 and III.ii.20.
218 *country* sexual;   having a cunt;   common *double entendres*.   See
      Partridge; and Marie Collins, 'Hamlet and the Lady's Lap', *Notes and
      Queries,* vol. 28 (1981), 130–2.
228–9 *tortures, besides the surgeon's.   Wine* ed.   (tortures; besides the
      Chirurgeon's Wine Q1–5, O).   The emended punctuation is supported
      by Wycherley's *Plays* (1720 and 1731 editions).   Markley suggests that
      besides the surgeon's is an afterthought suggested by Dorilant and
      Harcourt's laughter.

makes us sleep; love breaks it.   230

DORILANT

By the world, he has reason, Harcourt.

HORNER

Wine makes –

DORILANT

Ay wine makes us – makes us princes; love makes us
beggars, poor rogues, i'gad – and wine –

HORNER

So there's one converted. No, no, love and wine, oil 235
and vinegar.

HARCOURT

I grant it; love will still be uppermost.

HORNER

Come, for my part I will have only those glorious,
manly pleasures of being very drunk and very slovenly.

Enter BOY

BOY

Master Sparkish is below, sir.   240

                                           [*Exit* BOY]

HARCOURT

What, my dear friend! A rogue that is fond of me, only
I think for abusing him.

DORILANT

No, he can no more think the men laugh at him than
that women jilt him, his opinion of himself is so good.

HORNER

Well, there's another pleasure by drinking I thought not 245
of; I shall lose his acquaintance, because he cannot
drink. And you know 'tis a very hard thing to be rid of
him, for he's one of those nauseous offerers at wit, who,

---

231 *he has reason* This translates *il a raison*, he is right. Perhaps Dorilant, as
his name suggests, is French or frenchified.

242 *abusing* See I.i.146.

246–7 *he cannot drink* like Dapperwit, the would-be wit in *Love in a Wood*.
Vincent tries to make him drink because 'there is no other way to silence
him' (I.ii.16–17).

like the worst fiddlers, run themselves into all
companies.   250

HARCOURT

One that by being in the company of men of sense
would pass for one.

HORNER

And may so to the short-sighted world, as a false jewel
amongst true ones is not discerned at a distance. His
company is as troublesome to us as a cuckold's when 255
you have a mind to his wife's.

HARCOURT

No, the rogue will not let us enjoy one another, but
ravishes our conversation, though he signifies no more
to't than Sir Martin Mar-all's gaping and awkward
thrumming upon the lute does to his man's voice and 260
music.

DORILANT

And to pass for a wit in town shows himself a fool every
night to us, that are guilty of the plot.

HORNER

Such wits as he are, to a company of reasonable men,
like rooks to the gamesters, who only fill a room at the 265
table, but are so far from contributing to the play that
they only serve to spoil the fancy of those that do.

DORILANT

Nay, they are used like rooks too, snubbed, checked,
and abused; yet the rogues will hang on.

HORNER

A pox on 'em, and all that force nature, and would be 270
still what she forbids 'em! Affectation is her greatest
monster.

HARCOURT

Most men are the contraries to that they would seem.

---

253 *short-sighted* Q2–5, O (short-sighed Q1)
259 *Sir Martin Mar-all* hero of Dryden's *The Feigned Innocence; or, Sir
      Martin Mar-all* (1667), who serenades his mistress in mime while his
      hidden servant sings and plays the lute. As usual Sir Martin mars
      all by continuing after his servant has finished.
263 *us, that are guilty of the plot* those of us who have conspired to
      encourage him
265 *rooks* victims of tricksters. See also I.i.52.
      room place
267 *fancy* pleasure
268 *checked* taunted
270–1 *would be still* persist in trying to be

Your bully, you see, is a coward with a long sword; the
little, humbly fawning physician with his ebony cane is 275
he that destroys men.

DORILANT

The usurer, a poor rogue possessed of mouldy bonds
and mortgages; and we they call spendthrifts are only
wealthy, who lay out his money upon daily new
purchases of pleasure.   280

HORNER

Ay, your arrantest cheat is your trustee or executor;
your jealous man,   the greatest cuckold;   your
churchman, the greatest atheist;   and your noisy, pert
rogue of a wit, the greatest fop, dullest ass, and worst
company; as you shall see, for here he comes.   285

Enter SPARKISH *to them*

SPARKISH

How is't, sparks, how is't? Well, faith, Harry, I must
rally thee a little, ha, ha, ha! upon the report in town of
thee, ha, ha, ha! I can't hold i'faith! Shall I speak?

HORNER

Yes, but you'll be so bitter then.

SPARKISH

Honest Dick and Frank here shall answer for me, I will 290
not be extreme bitter, by the universe.

HARCOURT

We will be bound in ten thousand pound bond, he shall
not be bitter at all.

DORILANT

Nor sharp, nor sweet.

HORNER

What, not downright insipid?   295

---

275 *ebony cane* usually carried by physicians at the time
278 *are only* are the only ones who are
282 *your jealous man, the greatest cuckold* explained by Horner at III.ii.58–61
286 *sparks* young men about town;   usually depreciatory.   See note on
     Sparkish, p. 4.
287 *rally* make fun of; a fashionable word. See II.i.155 and note.
291 *extreme* extremely

SPARKISH

Nay then, since you are so brisk and provoke me, take
what follows. You must know, I was discoursing and
rallying with some ladies yesterday, and they happened
to talk of the fine new signs in town.

HORNER

Very fine ladies, I believe.   300

SPARKISH

Said I, 'I know where the best new sign is'. 'Where?'
says one of the ladies. 'In Covent Garden', I replied.
Said another, 'In what street?'   'In Russell Street',
answered I.   'Lord', says another, 'I'm sure there was
ne'er a fine new sign there yesterday'. 'Yes, but there 305
was', said I again, 'and it came out of France, and has
been there a fortnight'.

DORILANT

A pox! I can hear no more, prithee.

HORNER

No, hear him out; let him tune his crowd a while.

HARCOURT

The worst music, the greatest preparation.   310

SPARKISH

Nay, faith, I'll make you laugh. 'It cannot be', says a
third lady. 'Yes, yes', quoth I again. Says a fourth lady –

HORNER

Look to't, we'll have no more ladies.

SPARKISH

No – then mark, mark, now. Said I to the fourth, 'Did
you never see Master Horner? He lodges in Russell 315
Street, and he's a sign of a man, you know, since he
came out of France!' He, ha, he!

HORNER

But the devil take me, if thine be the sign of a jest.

---

296 *brisk* smart; depreciatory. In Etherege's *The Man of Mode* (1676) Sir
     Fopling Flutter is 'the gay, the giddy, brisk, insipid, noisy fool'
     (V.i.95–6); in *Pilgrim's Progress* (1678) Ignorance is 'a very brisk lad'
     from 'the country of Conceit'.
299 *signs* tradesmen's signs or symbols. See III.ii.202.
302 *Covent Garden* then a fashionable part of London, with some well-known
     taverns and coffee houses
303 *Russell Street* off the east side of Covent Garden
306 *again* in reply
309 *crowd* fiddle; perhaps a quibble on the more familiar sense, as Sparkish
     seems to know a lot of ladies
316 *sign* mere semblance

SPARKISH

    With that they all fell a-laughing, till they bepissed
    themselves. What, but it does not move you, methinks? 320
    Well, I see one had as good go to law without a witness,
    as break a jest without a laugher on one's side. Come,
    come sparks, but where do we dine? I have left at
    Whitehall an earl, to dine with you.

DORILANT

    Why, I thought thou hadst loved a man with a title 325
    better than a suit with a French trimming to't.

HARCOURT

    Go to him again.

SPARKISH

    No, sir, a wit to me is the greatest title in the world.

HORNER

    But go dine with your earl, sir; he may be exceptious.
    We are your friends, and will not take it ill to be left, I 330
    do assure you.

HARCOURT

    Nay, faith, he shall go to him.

SPARKISH

    Nay, pray, gentlemen.

DORILANT

    We'll thrust you out, if you won't. What, disappoint
    anybody for us?   335

SPARKISH

    Nay, dear gentlemen, hear me.

HORNER

    No, no sir, by no means; pray go, sir.

SPARKISH

    Why, dear rogues –

DORILANT

    No, no.   *They all thrust him out of the room*

ALL

    Ha, ha, ha!   340

321 *I* Q3, O (*omitted*, Q1–2, 4–5)
321–2 i.e., a joke needs someone to laugh at it, as a lawsuit needs a witness
326 *suit with a French trimming* fashionable suit;   unlikely to refer also to
    Horner's supposed impotence, as Dorilant is supporting him against
    Sparkish
327 *Go to him again* Q2–5, O (Go, to him again Q1). Holland defends Q1 as
    meaning Harcourt urges Dorilant to tease Sparkish further; but if so
    Dorilant ignores him, and Harcourt again urges Sparkish to return to the
    Earl in his next speech.
329 *exceptious* peevish

SPARKISH returns

SPARKISH

But, sparks, pray hear me. What, d'ye think I'll eat,
then, with gay shallow fops and silent coxcombs? I think
wit as necessary at dinner as a glass of good wine, and
that's the reason I never have any stomach when I eat
alone. Come, but where do we dine?   345

HORNER

Even where you will.

SPARKISH

At Chateline's?

DORILANT

Yes, if you will.

SPARKISH

Or at the Cock?

DORILANT

Yes, if you please.   350

SPARKISH

Or at the Dog and Partridge?

HORNER

Ay, if you have a mind to't, for we shall dine at neither.

SPARKISH

Pshaw! with your fooling we shall lose the new play.
And I would no more miss seeing a new play the first
day than I would miss sitting in the wits' row. Therefore 355
I'll go fetch my mistress and away.

Exit SPARKISH

Manent HORNER, HARCOURT, DORILANT. *Enter to them*
PINCHWIFE

HORNER

Who have we here? Pinchwife!

---

344 *stomach* appetite
347 *Chateline's* French restaurant in Covent Garden
349 *the Cock* probably the tavern in Bow Street, Covent Garden.
    Wycherley went there, and set *The Plain Dealer* V.ii there.
351 *the Dog and Partridge* tavern in Fleet Street; probably the least
    acceptable of Sparkish's suggestions
352 *a mind* Q2-5, O (mind Q1)
    neither none of them (*OED* B. 2.c)
355 *sitting* Q3 (setting Q1-2, 4-5, O)
    the wits' row with other wits, in the pit
356 sd *manent* remain

PINCHWIFE
Gentlemen, your humble servant.

HORNER
Well, Jack, by thy long absence from the town, the
grumness of thy countenance, and the slovenliness of   360
thy habit, I should give thee joy, should I not, of
marriage?

PINCHWIFE (*Aside*)
Death! does he know I'm married too? I thought to
have concealed it from him at least. – My long stay in
the country will excuse my dress, and I have a suit of   365
law, that brings me up to town, that puts me out of
humour. Besides, I must give Sparkish tomorrow five
thousand pound to lie with my sister.

HORNER
Nay, you country gentlemen, rather than not purchase,
will buy anything; and he is a cracked title, if we may   370
quibble. Well, but am I to give thee joy? I heard thou
wert married.

PINCHWIFE
What then?

HORNER
Why, the next thing that is to be heard is, thou'rt a
cuckold.   375

PINCHWIFE (*Aside*)
Insupportable name!

HORNER
But I did not expect marriage from such a whoremaster
as you, one that knew the town so much, and women so
well.

PINCHWIFE
Why, I have married no London wife.   380

HORNER
Pshaw! that's all one. That grave circumspection in
marrying a country wife is like refusing a deceitful,

360 *grumness* moroseness. Don Diego, in *The Gentleman Dancing Master*,
     boasts of being 'grum, and jealous' (II.i.36).
367–8 *five thousand pound* as a dowry. Pinchwife must be wealthy.
369 *purchase* acquire land or property by purchase
370 *cracked title* a property in a poor state of repair, or bankrupt, or (as
     applied to Sparkish) 'cracked'. He is a bad buy.
377 *whoremaster* experienced lecher
378 *one that knew the town so much* Horner ridicules Pinchwife's claim before
     he has even made it; see ll. 438, 458. Later, Dorilant ridicules it too;
     see ll. 477–8.

pampered Smithfield jade, to go and be cheated by a
friend in the country.

PINCHWIFE (*Aside*)

A pox on him and his simile! – At least we are a little   385
surer of the breed there, know what her keeping has
been, whether foiled or unsound.

HORNER

Come, come, I have known a clap gotten in Wales. And
there are cozens, justices, clerks, and chaplains in the
country; I won't say coachmen! But she's handsome   390
and young?

PINCHWIFE (*Aside*)

I'll answer as I should do. – No, no, she has no beauty
but her youth; no attraction but her modesty; whole-
some, homely, and housewifely, that's all.

DORILANT

He talks as like a grazier as he looks.   395

PINCHWIFE

She's too awkward, ill-favoured, and silly to bring to
town.

---

383 *Smithfield* horse market with reputation for sharp practice: 'This town
two bargains has, not worth one farthing, / A Smithfield horse, and a
wife of Covent-Garden' (Dryden, *The Kind Keeper* (1680),
Epilogue).
jade both worn-out horse and disreputable woman

386 *keeping* how she has been kept; *double entendre*. See I.i.460 and note.

387 *foiled* both injured (horse) and deflowered (woman)
unsound diseased

388 *clap* gonorrhoea
Wales to Londoners a remote part of the country

389 *cozens* cozeners, cheaters; needlessly altered to 'cousins' by some
editors. Horner has mentioned cheating at l. 383.
justices, clerks, Q1 (justices clerks, Q2-5, O). Q1 adds one to
Horner's list of supposedly respectable people who spread venereal
disease.

390 *coachmen* legendary studs. Dapperwit regards Lady Flippant's
coachman as his rival (*Love in a Wood* I.ii.232–3); Mrs Caution is
accused of having fancied her father's coachman (*The Gentleman
Dancing-Master* I.i.319).

392 *as I should do* perhaps 'as you would expect'; we expect lies. This
was altered in Lee's *The Country Wife* to 'I'll answer him accordingly'
and cut in Garrick's *The Country Girl*.

395 *grazier* one who fattens cattle for the market

396 *silly* ignorant

HARCOURT

Then methinks you should bring her, to be taught breeding.

PINCHWIFE

To be taught! No, sir, I thank you. Good wives and 400 private soldiers should be ignorant. [*Aside*] I'll keep her from your instructions, I warrant you.

HARCOURT (*Aside*)

The rogue is as jealous as if his wife were not ignorant.

HORNER

Why, if she be ill-favoured, there will be less danger here for you than by leaving her in the country. We have such 405 variety of dainties that we are seldom hungry.

DORILANT

But they have always coarse, constant, swingeing stomachs in the country.

HARCOURT

Foul feeders indeed.

DORILANT

And your hospitality is great there.   410

HARCOURT

Open house, every man's welcome!

PINCHWIFE

So, so, gentlemen.

HORNER

But, prithee, why would'st thou marry her? If she be ugly, ill-bred, and silly, she must be rich then?

PINCHWIFE

As rich as if she brought me twenty thousand pound out 415 of this town; for she'll be as sure not to spend her moderate portion as a London baggage would be to spend hers, let it be what it would; so 'tis all one. Then, because she's ugly, she's the likelier to be my own; and being ill-bred, she'll hate conversation; and since silly 420 and innocent, will not know the difference betwixt a man of one-and-twenty and one of forty.

---

398 sp *HARCOURT* (*Har.* Q1-5, O). But the Q1 reading could be a printer's error for *Hor.*, i.e., Horner; Pinchwife's next aside refers to Horner rather than Harcourt.

    breeding gentility and, probably, pregnancy

403 sd (*Aside*) Q1-5, O. But the line need not be spoken aside, so perhaps the sd is meant for Pinchwife's aside at ll. 401-2.

407-8 *swingeing stomachs* huge appetites

418 *'tis all one* it's as if she had brought me a fortune

HORNER

> Nine – to my knowledge; but if she be silly, she'll expect
> as much from a man of forty-nine as from him of one-
> and-twenty. But methinks wit is more necessary than 425
> beauty; and I think no young woman ugly that has it,
> and no handsome woman agreeable without it.

PINCHWIFE

> 'Tis my maxim, he's a fool that marries, but he's a
> greater that does not marry a fool. What is wit in a wife
> good for, but to make a man a cuckold?   430

HORNER

> Yes, to keep it from his knowledge.

PINCHWIFE

> A fool cannot contrive to make her husband a cuckold.

HORNER

> No, but she'll club with a man that can; and what is
> worse, if she cannot make her husband a cuckold, she'll
> make him jealous, and pass for one, and then 'tis all one. 435

PINCHWIFE

> Well, well, I'll take care for one, my wife shall make me
> no cuckold, though she had your help, Master Horner;
> I understand the town, sir.

DORILANT (*Aside*)

> His help!

HARCOURT (*Aside*)

> He's come newly to town, it seems, and has not heard 440
> how things are with him.

HORNER

> But tell me, has marriage cured thee of whoring, which
> it seldom does?

HARCOURT

> 'Tis more than age can do.

HORNER

> No, the word is, I'll marry and live honest. But a 445
> marriage vow is like a penitent gamester's oath, and
> entering into bonds and penalties to stint himself to such
> a particular small sum at play for the future, which
> makes him but the more eager, and not being able to

---

433 *club* get together
445 *word* usual saying
    honest chaste
448 *such* such and such
    play gambling

hold out, loses his money again, and his forfeit to boot.   450
DORILANT
Ay, ay, a gamester will be a gamester whilst his money
lasts, and a whoremaster, whilst his vigour.
HARCOURT
Nay, I have known 'em, when they are broke and can
lose no more, keep a-fumbling with the box in their
hands to fool with only, and hinder other gamesters.   455
DORILANT
That had wherewithal to make lusty stakes.
PINCHWIFE
Well, gentlemen, you may laugh at me, but you shall
never lie with my wife; I know the town.
HORNER
But prithee, was not the way you were in better? Is not
keeping better than marriage?   460
PINCHWIFE
A pox on't! The jades would jilt me; I could never keep
a whore to myself.
HORNER
So, then, you only married to keep a whore to yourself.
Well, but let me tell you, women, as you say, are like
soldiers, made constant and loyal by good pay rather   465
than by oaths and covenants. Therefore I'd advise my
friends to keep rather than marry, since too I find, by
your example, it does not serve one's turn; for I saw you
yesterday in the eighteen-penny place with a pretty
country wench!   470
PINCHWIFE (*Aside*)
How the devil! Did he see my wife then? I sat there that
she might not be seen. But she shall never go to a play
again.

450 *hold out* keep to his plan
     forfeit payment under the 'bonds and penalties'
454 *box* both receptacle for dice and vagina; noted in *Modern Language
     Review*, vol. 82 (1987), 31 by Ian Donaldson, who draws attention to the
     source in Horace, *Satires* 2.7. 15–18, and to similar ideas in Rochester,
     'The Disabled Debauchee' (*c.* 1675)
456 *lusty stakes* big bets and, probably, erections. Some such *double entendre*
     is needed to complete the analogy between a gambler and a lecher, and
     to explain the wits' laughter.
460 *keeping* supporting a mistress. See also I.i.386.
469 *eighteen-penny place* the middle gallery in the theatre, the best place for a
     man to stop his wife being seen by the gallants in the pit and the boxes.
     But it was also frequented by prostitutes.

HORNER

What, dost thou blush at nine-and-forty for having been
seen with a wench?   475

DORILANT

No, faith, I warrant 'twas his wife, which he seated there
out of sight, for he's a cunning rogue, and understands
the town.

HARCOURT

He blushes! Then 'twas his wife; for men are now
more ashamed to be seen with them in public than with 480
a wench.

PINCHWIFE (*Aside*)

Hell and damnation! I'm undone, since Horner has
seen her, and they know 'twas she.

HORNER

But prithee, was it thy wife? She was exceedingly
pretty; I was in love with her at that distance.   485

PINCHWIFE

You are like never to be nearer to her. Your servant,
gentlemen.   *Offers to go*

HORNER

Nay, prithee stay.

PINCHWIFE

I cannot, I will not.

HORNER

Come, you shall dine with us.   490

PINCHWIFE

I have dined already.

HORNER

Come, I know thou hast not. I'll treat thee, dear rogue.
Thou shan't spend none of thy Hampshire money
today.

PINCHWIFE (*Aside*)

Treat me! So, he uses me already like his cuckold!   495

HORNER

Nay, you shall not go.

PINCHWIFE

I must, I have business at home.

Exit PINCHWIFE

---

487 sd *offers* attempts
492 *rogue* term of endearment as well as abuse
493 *Hampshire* the country (antonomasia), or Horner may know Pinchwife
     now lives there. See II.i.118.
495 See IV.iii.269–70.

HARCOURT

To beat his wife! He's as jealous of her as a Cheapside
husband of a Covent Garden wife.

HORNER

Why, 'tis as hard to find an old whoremaster without 500
jealousy and the gout, as a young one without fear or the
pox.

As gout in age from pox in youth proceeds,
So wenching past, then jealousy succeeds;
The worst disease that love and wenching breeds.   505

[Exeunt]

Act II, Scene i

MRS MARGERY PINCHWIFE *and* ALITHEA, PINCHWIFE
peeping behind at the door

MRS PINCHWIFE

Pray, sister, where are the best fields and woods to walk
in, in London?

ALITHEA

A pretty question! Why, sister, Mulberry Garden and St
James's Park; and for close walks, the New Exchange.

MRS PINCHWIFE

Pray, sister, tell me why my husband looks so grum here   5
in town, and keeps me up so close, and will not let me
go a-walking, nor let me wear my best gown yesterday?

ALITHEA

Oh, he's jealous, sister.

MRS PINCHWIFE

Jealous? What's that?

ALITHEA

He's afraid you should love another man.   10

498–9 *Cheapside husband* bourgeois husband
499 *Covent Garden wife* upper class wife. For Dryden's opinion of such
     wives, see I.i.383 note.
  3–4 *Mulberry Garden and St James's Park* fashionable meeting places;
     settings for scenes in *Love in a Wood*. The garden was in the park, where
     Buckingham Palace now stands.
  4 *close* covered
     New Exchange arcade with fasionable shops; setting for III.ii
  5 *grum* morose. He makes the same impression on Horner, I.i.360.
  6 *up so close* so closely confined

MRS PINCHWIFE

How should he be afraid of my loving another man,
when he will not let me see any but himself?

ALITHEA

Did he not carry you yesterday to a play?

MRS PINCHWIFE

Ay, but we sat amongst ugly people. He would not let
me come near the gentry, who sat under us, so that I   15
could not see 'em. He told me none but naughty
women sat there, whom they toused and moused. But I
would have ventured for all that.

ALITHEA

But how did you like the play?

MRS PINCHWIFE

Indeed I was a-weary of the play, but I liked hugeously   20
the actors! They are the goodliest, properest men, sister.

ALITHEA

Oh, but you must not like the actors, sister.

MRS PINCHWIFE

Ay, how should I help it, sister? Pray, sister, when my
husband comes in, will you ask leave for me to go a-
walking?   25

ALITHEA (*Aside*)

A-walking! Ha, ha! Lord, a country gentlewoman's
leisure is the drudgery of a foot-post; and she requires
as much airing as her husband's horses.

Enter PINCHWIFE *to them*

But here comes your husband; I'll ask, though I'm sure
he'll not grant it.   30

MRS PINCHWIFE

He says he won't let me go abroad for fear of catching
the pox.

ALITHEA

Fie, the smallpox you should say.

MRS PINCHWIFE

Oh my dear, dear bud, welcome home! Why dost thou

13 *carry* take
17 *toused and moused* tousled and mousled, engaged in sexual harrassment
    (*OED* mouse *v.* 3.b; Farmer and Henley, tousle)
20 *hugeously* 'terrifically'; vulgarism
21 *properest* most handsome
27 *foot-post* messenger on foot
34 *bud* term of endearment usually applied to children. But in Garrick's

look so froppish? Who has nangered thee?   35
PINCHWIFE
You're a fool!   MRS PINCHWIFE *goes aside and cries*
ALITHEA
Faith, so she is, for crying for no fault, poor tender
creature!
PINCHWIFE
What, you would have her as impudent as yourself, as
arrant a jill-flirt, a gadder, a magpie, and – to say all – a   40
mere notorious town-woman?
ALITHEA
Brother, you are my only censurer; and the honour of
your family shall sooner suffer in your wife there than in
me, though I take the innocent liberty of the town.
PINCHWIFE
Hark you, mistress, do not talk so before my wife. The   45
innocent liberty of the town!
ALITHEA
Why, pray, who boasts of any intrigue with me? What
lampoon has made my name notorious?   What ill
women frequent my lodgings? I keep no company with
any women of scandalous reputations.   50
PINCHWIFE
No, you keep the men of scandalous reputations
company.
ALITHEA
Where? Would you not have me civil? Answer 'em in a
box at the plays, in the drawing room at Whitehall, in St
James's Park, Mulberry Garden, or –   55
PINCHWIFE
Hold, hold! Do not teach my wife where the men are to
be found!   I believe she's the worse for your town
documents already. I bid you keep her in ignorance, as
I do.

The Country Girl Lucy says 'Bud means husband … and if he was my
husband I'd bud him, a surly, unreasonable beast' (II.ii). Perhaps
Wycherley alludes to the cuckold's budding horns.
35 *froppish* fretful; *nangered* angered. Again she talks to him as if he were a
    child.
40 *jill-flirt* wanton girl
    gadder gadabout
    magpie chatterer
48 *lampoon* scurrilous satire circulating in manuscript
57–8 *town documents* lessons about the town

MRS PINCHWIFE

Indeed, be not angry with her, bud. She will tell me   60
nothing of the town though I ask her a thousand times a
day.

PINCHWIFE

Then you are very inquisitive to know, I find!

MRS PINCHWIFE

Not I, indeed, dear. I hate London. Our placehouse in
the country is worth a thousand of't. Would I were   65
there again!

PINCHWIFE

So you shall, I warrant. But were you not talking of
plays and players when I came in? [*To* ALITHEA] You
are her encourager in such discourses.

MRS PINCHWIFE

No, indeed, dear; she chid me just now for liking the   70
player-men.

PINCHWIFE (*Aside*)

Nay, if she be so innocent as to own to me her liking
them, there is no hurt in't. – Come, my poor rogue, but
thou lik'st none better than me?

MRS PINCHWIFE

Yes, indeed, but I do; the player-men are finer folks.   75

PINCHWIFE

But you love none better than me?

MRS PINCHWIFE

You are mine own dear bud, and I know you; I hate a
stranger.

PINCHWIFE

Ay, my dear, you must love me only, and not be like the
naughty town-women, who only hate their husbands   80
and love every man else; love plays, visits, fine coaches,
fine clothes, fiddles, balls, treats, and so lead a wicked
town-life.

MRS PINCHWIFE

Nay, if to enjoy all these things be a town-life, London is
not so bad a place, dear.   85

64 *placehouse* chief house on an estate. Suggests a wealthy background.
71 *player-men* actors, as she called them at II.i.21;   perhaps childish
    language, for Pinchwife's benefit
82 *fiddles* fiddlers
    balls social gatherings
    treats entertainments

PINCHWIFE

How! If you love me, you must hate London.

ALITHEA [*Aside*]

The fool has forbid me discovering to her the pleasures
of the town, and he is now setting her agog upon them
himself.

MRS PINCHWIFE

But, husband, do the town-women love the player-men   90
too?

PINCHWIFE

Yes, I warrant you.

MRS PINCHWIFE

Ay, I warrant you.

PINCHWIFE

Why, you do not, I hope?

MRS PINCHWIFE

No, no, bud; but why have we no player-men in the   95
country?

PINCHWIFE

Ha! – Mistress Minx, ask me no more to go to a play.

MRS PINCHWIFE

Nay, why love? I did not care for going, but when you
forbid me, you make me, as't were, desire it.

ALITHEA (*Aside*)

So 'twill be in other things, I warrant.   100

MRS PINCHWIFE

Pray, let me go to a play, dear.

PINCHWIFE

Hold your peace, I won't.

MRS PINCHWIFE

Why, love?

PINCHWIFE

Why, I'll tell you.

ALITHEA (*Aside*)

Nay, if he tell her, she'll give him more cause to forbid 105
her that place.

MRS PINCHWIFE

Pray, why, dear?

PINCHWIFE

First, you like the actors, and the gallants may like you.

---

88 *setting her agog upon* making her eager for
93 sp MRS PINCHWIFE Q1–5, O. Gamini Salgado assigns this speech to
    Alithea (*Three Restoration Comedies*, 1968). But if Mrs Pinchwife has it
    Pinchwife's question (l. 94) makes better sense.

MRS PINCHWIFE

What, a homely country girl? No, bud, nobody will like
me.   110

PINCHWIFE

I tell you, yes, they may.

MRS PINCHWIFE

No, no, you jest – I won't believe you, I will go.

PINCHWIFE

I tell you then, that one of the lewdest fellows in town,
who saw you there, told me he was in love with you.

MRS PINCHWIFE

Indeed! Who, who, pray who was't?   115

PINCHWIFE *(Aside)*

I've gone too far, and slipped before I was aware. How
overjoyed she is!

MRS PINCHWIFE

Was it any Hampshire gallant, any of our neighbours? I
promise you, I am beholding to him.

PINCHWIFE

I promise you, you lie; for he would but ruin you, as he 120
has done hundreds. He has no other love for women,
but that; such as he look upon women like basilisks, but
to destroy 'em.

MRS PINCHWIFE

Ay, but if he loves me, why should he ruin me? Answer
me to that. Methinks he should not; I would do him no 125
harm.

ALITHEA

Ha, ha, ha!

PINCHWIFE

'Tis very well; but I'll keep him from doing you any
harm, or me either.

Enter SPARKISH *and* HARCOURT

But here comes company; get you in, get you in.   130

MRS PINCHWIFE

But pray, husband, is he a pretty gentleman that loves
me?

PINCHWIFE

In, baggage, in! *(Thrusts her in; shuts the door)* [*Aside*]
What, all the lewd libertines of the town brought to my

---

119 *beholding* beholden
122 *like basilisks* as basilisks do, a basilisk being a fabulous reptile whose
glance was fatal

lodging by this easy coxcomb! 'Sdeath, I'll not suffer it.   135

SPARKISH

Here Harcourt, do you approve my choice?   [*To*
ALITHEA] Dear little rogue, I told you I'd bring you
acquainted with all my friends, the wits, and –

                                        HARCOURT *salutes her*

PINCHWIFE [*Aside*]

Ay, they shall know her, as well as you yourself will, I
warrant you.   140

SPARKISH

This is one of those, my pretty rogue, that are to dance
at your wedding tomorrow;   and him you must bid
welcome ever to what you and I have.

PINCHWIFE (*Aside*)

Monstrous!

SPARKISH

Harcourt, how dost thou like her, faith? – Nay, dear, do 145
not look down; I should hate to have a wife of mine out
of countenance at anything.

PINCHWIFE [*Aside*]

Wonderful!

SPARKISH

Tell me, I say, Harcourt, how dost thou like her? Thou
hast stared upon her enough to resolve me.   150

HARCOURT

So infinitely well that I could wish I had a mistress too,
that might differ from her in nothing but her love and
engagement to you.

ALITHEA

Sir, Master Sparkish has often told me that his
acquaintance were all wits and railleurs, and now I find   155
it.

SPARKISH

No, by the universe madam, he does not rally now; you
may believe him, I do assure you, he is the honestest,
worthiest, true-hearted gentleman – a man of such
perfect honour, he would say nothing to a lady he does   160
not mean.

PINCHWIFE [*Aside*]

Praising another man to his mistress!

---

135 *easy coxcomb* easy-going fop
150 *resolve me* give me your opinion
155 *railleurs* railers, mockers; fashionable French word likely to have been
      used by Sparkish. See I.i.287.

HARCOURT

Sir, you are so beyond expectation obliging, that –

SPARKISH

Nay, i'gad, I am sure you do admire her extremely; I
see't in your eyes. – He does admire you, madam. – By 165
the world, don't you?

HARCOURT

Yes, above the world, or the most glorious part of it, her
whole sex; and till now I never thought I should have
envied you or any man about to marry, but you have the
best excuse for marriage I ever knew.   170

ALITHEA

Nay, now, sir, I'm satisfied you are of the society of the
wits and railleurs since you cannot spare your friend
even when he is but too civil to you. But the surest sign
is, since you are an enemy to marriage; for that, I hear,
you hate as much as business or bad wine.   175

HARCOURT

Truly, madam, I never was an enemy to marriage till
now, because marriage was never an enemy to me
before.

ALITHEA

But why, sir, is marriage an enemy to you now? Because
it robs you of your friend here? For you look upon a 180
friend married as one gone into a monastery, that is
dead to the world.

HARCOURT

'Tis indeed, because you marry him; I see, madam, you
can guess my meaning. I do confess heartily and openly,
I wish it were in my power to break the match. By 185
heavens I would!

SPARKISH

Poor Frank!

ALITHEA

Would you be so unkind to me?

HARCOURT

No, no, 'tis not because I would be unkind to you.

SPARKISH

Poor Frank! No, gad, 'tis only his kindness to me.   190

173–5 Raillery against marriage was so common among the wits as to have
become unfashionable; Friedman quotes Thomas Shadwell, *The Miser*
(1672), where Bellmour complains of Hazard that he has 'the common
place wit of all the young fops in this town, in railing against marriage'.

PINCHWIFE (*Aside*)

Great kindness to you indeed! Insensible fop, let a man make love to his wife to his face!

SPARKISH

Come, dear Frank, for all my wife there that shall be, thou shalt enjoy me sometimes, dear rogue. By my honour, we men of wit condole for our deceased brother 195 in marriage as much as for one dead in earnest. – I think that was prettily said of me, ha, Harcourt? – But come, Frank, be not melancholy for me.

HARCOURT

No, I assure you I am not melancholy for you.

SPARKISH

Prithee, Frank, dost think my wife that shall be, there, a 200 fine person?

HARCOURT

I could gaze upon her till I became as blind as you are.

SPARKISH

How, as I am? How?

HARCOURT

Because you are a lover, and true lovers are blind, stock blind. 205

SPARKISH

True, true; but by the world, she has wit too, as well as beauty. Go, go with her into a corner, and try if she has wit; talk to her anything; she's bashful before me.

HARCOURT

Indeed, if a woman wants wit in a corner, she has it nowhere. 210

ALITHEA (*Aside to* SPARKISH)

Sir, you dispose of me a little before your time –

SPARKISH

Nay, nay, madam, let me have an earnest of your

194 *enjoy me* have the pleasure of my company
198 *not* Q2–5, O (not not Q1)
204–5 *stock blind* as blind as a lifeless thing or stupid person (*OED* stock *sb.*¹ VIII.60)
209 *wit in a corner* i.e., perhaps, impudence in an assignation. In *Love in a Wood* Lady Flippant complains 'I do not know a man of you all, that will not thrust a woman up into a corner, and then talk an hour to her impertinently of marriage', and Ranger assures her 'You would find me another man in a corner' (I.ii.261–4). A distant echo of Horace, *Odes*, 'gratus puellae risus ab angulo' (1.9.22), the agreeable laughter of a girl from a corner.
212 *earnest* foretaste

obedience or – Go, go, madam –

> HARCOURT *courts* ALITHEA *aside*

PINCHWIFE

How, sir! If you are not concerned for the honour of a
wife, I am for that of a sister; he shall not debauch her. 215
Be a pander to your own wife, bring men to her, let 'em
make love before your face, thrust 'em into a corner
together, then leave 'em in private! Is this your town wit
and conduct?

SPARKISH

Ha, ha, ha! A silly wise rogue would make one laugh 220
more than a stark fool, ha, ha! I shall burst. Nay, you
shall not disturb 'em; I'll vex thee, by the world.

> *Struggles with* PINCHWIFE *to keep him*
> *from* HARCOURT *and* ALITHEA

ALITHEA

The writings are drawn, sir, settlements made; 'tis too
late, sir, and past all revocation.

HARCOURT

Then so is my death.   225

ALITHEA

I would not be unjust to him.

HARCOURT

Then why to me so?

ALITHEA

I have no obligation to you.

HARCOURT

My love.

ALITHEA

I had his before.   230

HARCOURT

You never had it; he wants, you see, jealousy, the only
infallible sign of it.

ALITHEA

Love proceeds from esteem; he cannot distrust my
virtue. Besides he loves me, or he would not marry me.

HARCOURT

Marrying you is no more sign of his love, than bribing 235
your woman, that he may marry you, is a sign of his

---

220 *would* who would
222 *vex* thwart
231–2 proverbial, and a recurrent idea in Wycherley. See *Love in a Wood*
      IV.iii.28–9.

generosity. Marriage is rather a sign of interest than
love; and he that marries a fortune, covets a mistress,
not loves her. But if you take marriage for a sign of love,
take it from me immediately.   240

ALITHEA

No, now you have put a scruple in my head. But in
short, sir, to end our dispute, I must marry him; my
reputation would suffer in the world else.

HARCOURT

No, if you do marry him, with your pardon, madam,
your reputation suffers in the world, and you would be 245
thought in necessity for a cloak.

ALITHEA

Nay, now you are rude, sir. – Master Sparkish, pray
come hither, your friend here is very troublesome, and
very loving.

HARCOURT (*Aside to* ALITHEA)

Hold, hold!   250

PINCHWIFE

D'ye hear that?

SPARKISH

Why, d'ye think I'll seem to be jealous, like a country
bumpkin?

PINCHWIFE

No, rather be a cuckold, like a credulous cit.

HARCOURT

Madam, you would not have been so little generous as 255
to have told him?

ALITHEA

Yes, since you could be so little generous as to wrong
him.

HARCOURT

Wrong him! No man can do't, he's beneath an injury; a
bubble, a coward, a senseless idiot, a wretch so 260
contemptible to all the world but you that –

---

237 *interest* self-interest
      than Q4–5, O (then Q1–3)
246 *cloak* cover for immorality. Cook and Swannell quote Aphra Behn, *The
      City Heiress* (1682): 'Would you have the impudence to marry an old
      coxcomb, a fellow that will not so much as serve you for a cloak, he is so
      visibly and undeniably impotent?' (II.iii). See also III.ii.190.
254 *cit* citizen; disparaging
260 *bubble* dupe. See also III.ii.64–72.

ALITHEA

Hold, do not rail at him, for since he is like to be my
husband I am resolved to like him. Nay, I think I am
obliged to tell him you are not his friend. – Master
Sparkish, Master Sparkish!   265

SPARKISH

What, what? Now, dear rogue, has not she wit?

HARCOURT (*Speaks surlily*)

Not so much as I thought, and hoped she had.

ALITHEA

Master Sparkish, do you bring people to rail at you?

HARCOURT

Madam –

SPARKISH

How! No, but if he does rail at me, 'tis but in jest, I   270
warrant;   what we wits do for one another and never
take any notice of it.

ALITHEA

He spoke so scurrilously of you, I had no patience to
hear him; besides, he has been making love to me.

HARCOURT (*Aside*)

True, damned, tell-tale woman.   275

SPARKISH

Pshaw! to show his parts. We wits rail and make love
often but to show our parts; as we have no affections, so
we have no malice; we –

ALITHEA

He said you were a wretch, below an injury.

SPARKISH

Pshaw!   280

HARCOURT [*Aside*]

Damned, senseless, impudent, virtuous jade! Well, since
she won't let me have her, she'll do as good, she'll make
me hate her.

ALITHEA

A common bubble.

SPARKISH

Pshaw!   285

ALITHEA

A coward.

276 *parts* (generally) talents, intellectual abilities; (to fops like Sparkish)
superficial accomplishments; (sometimes) private parts. The bawdy
double entendre follows at ll. 277 and 289–90, but maybe Sparkish does
not know what he is saying, like Sir Jaspar Fidget at II.i.602 and
IV.iii.105, 148–9.

SPARKISH

Pshaw, pshaw!

ALITHEA

A senseless, drivelling idiot.

SPARKISH

How! Did he disparage my parts? Nay, then my
honour's concerned. I can't put up that, sir, by the 290
world. Brother, help me to kill him. (*Aside*) I may draw
now, since we have the odds of him. 'Tis a good
occasion, too, before my mistress –   *Offers to draw*

ALITHEA

Hold, hold!

SPARKISH

What, what?   295

ALITHEA (*Aside*)

I must not let 'em kill the gentleman neither, for his
kindness to me; I am so far from hating him that I wish
my gallant had his person and understanding. – Nay, if
my honour

SPARKISH

I'll be thy death.   300

ALITHEA

Hold, hold! Indeed, to tell the truth, the gentleman said
after all that what he spoke was but out of friendship to
you.

SPARKISH

How! say, I am – I am a fool, that is no wit, out of
friendship to me?   305

ALITHEA

Yes, to try whether I was concerned enough for you, and
made love to me only to be satisfied of my virtue, for
your sake.

HARCOURT (*Aside*)

Kind, however –

SPARKISH

Nay, if it were so, my dear rogue, I ask thee pardon. But 310
why would not you tell me so, faith?

HARCOURT

Because I did not think on't, faith.

---

289 *disparage my parts* criticise my intellectual powers, 'say … I am a fool,
        that is no wit' (l. 304)
290 *put up* put up with
302 *after all* in conclusion

SPARKISH

Come, Horner does not come. Harcourt, let's be gone
to the new play. – Come, madam.

ALITHEA

I will not go, if you intend to leave me alone in the box 315
and run into the pit, as you use to do.

SPARKISH

Pshaw!   I'll leave Harcourt with you in the box to
entertain you and that's as good. If I sat in the box I
should be thought no judge but of trimmings. – Come
away, Harcourt, lead her down.   320

Exeunt SPARKISH, HARCOURT *and* ALITHEA

PINCHWIFE

Well, go thy ways, for the flower of the true town fops,
such as spend their estates before they come to 'em, and
are cuckolds before they're married. But let me go look
to my own freehold – How!

Enter my LADY FIDGET, *Mrs* DAINTY FIDGET
and Mrs SQUEAMISH

LADY FIDGET

Your servant, sir. Where is your lady? We are come to 325
wait upon her to the new play.

PINCHWIFE

New play!

LADY FIDGET

And my husband will wait upon you presently.

PINCHWIFE (*Aside*)

Damn your civility. – Madam, by no means; I will not
see Sir Jaspar here till I have waited upon him at home; 330
nor shall my wife see you till she has waited upon your
ladyship at your lodgings.

LADY FIDGET

Now we are here, sir –

PINCHWIFE

No, madam.

DAINTY

Pray let us see her.   335

SQUEAMISH

We will not stir till we see her.

---

315 *box* one of a number of private boxes in the theatre gallery
316 *pit* where 'the wits' row' (I.i.355) was
319 *trimmings* probably, fashionable adornments. See I.i.326.
320 *lead her down* give her your arm   324 *freehold* i.e. his wife

PINCHWIFE (*Aside*)

A pox on you all! (*Goes to the door and returns*) She has
locked the door, and is gone abroad.

LADY FIDGET

No, you have locked the door, and she's within.

DAINTY

They told us below, she was here.   340

PINCHWIFE [*Aside*]

Will nothing do? – Well, it must out then. To tell you
the truth, ladies, which I was afraid to let you know
before, lest it might endanger your lives, my wife has just
now the small-pox come out upon her. Do not be
frightened; but pray, be gone, ladies; you shall not stay 345
here in danger of your lives; pray get you gone, ladies.

LADY FIDGET

No, no, we have all had 'em.

SQUEAMISH

Alack, alack!

DAINTY

Come, come, we must see how it goes with her; I
understand the disease.   350

LADY FIDGET

Come.

PINCHWIFE (*Aside*)

Well, there is no being too hard for women at their own
weapon, lying; therefore I'll quit the field.

Exit PINCHWIFE

SQUEAMISH

Here's an example of jealousy!

LADY FIDGET

Indeed, as the world goes, I wonder there are no more 355
jealous, since wives are so neglected.

DAINTY

Pshaw! as the world goes, to what end should they be
jealous?

LADY FIDGET

Foh! 'tis a nasty world.

SQUEAMISH

That men of parts, great acquaintance, and quality 360
should take up with and spend themselves and fortunes
in keeping little playhouse creatures, foh!

360–2 Nell Gwyn was only the most famous actress who took up such an
offer. See also Prologue, ll. 27–8.

LADY FIDGET
  Nay, that women of understanding, great acquaintance
  and good quality should fall a-keeping, too, of little
  creatures, foh!   365
SQUEAMISH
  Why, 'tis the men of quality's fault. They never visit
  women of honour and reputation as they used to do;
  and have not so much as common civility for ladies of
  our rank, but use us with the same indifferency and ill-
  breeding as if we were all married to 'em.   370
LADY FIDGET
  She says true! 'Tis an arrant shame women of quality
  should be so slighted. Methinks, birth – birth should go
  for something. I have known men admired, courted,
  and followed for their titles only.
SQUEAMISH
  Ay, one would think men of honour should not love, no   375
  more than marry, out of their own rank.
DAINTY
  Fie, fie upon 'em! They are come to think cross-
  breeding for themselves best, as well as for their dogs
  and horses.
LADY FIDGET
  They are dogs, and horses for't.   380
SQUEAMISH
  One would think, if not for love, for vanity a little.
DAINTY
  Nay, they do satisfy their vanity upon us sometimes,
  and are kind to us in their report; tell all the world they
  lie with us.
LADY FIDGET
  Damned rascals! That we should be only wronged by   385
  'em. To report a man has had a person, when he has
  not had a person, is the greatest wrong in the whole
  world that can be done to a person.
SQUEAMISH
  Well, 'tis an arrant shame noble persons should be so
  wronged and neglected.   390

363–5 For instance, Lady Castlemaine had liaisons with both Charles Hart
   and Wycherley himself.
369 *indifferency* indifference
375–6 *love, no more than marry,* ed. (love no more, than marry Q1-5, O)
380 *for't* for thinking it.

LADY FIDGET
But still 'tis an arranter shame for a noble person to
neglect her own honour, and defame her own noble
person with little inconsiderable fellows, foh!
DAINTY
I suppose the crime against our honour is the same with
a man of quality as with another.   395
LADY FIDGET
How! No, sure, the man of quality is likest one's
husband and therefore the fault should be the less.
DAINTY
But then the pleasure should be the less.
LADY FIDGET
Fie, fie, fie, for shame, sister! Whither shall we ramble?
Be continent in your discourse, or I shall hate you.   400
DAINTY
Besides, an intrigue is so much the more notorious for
the man's quality.
SQUEAMISH
'Tis true, nobody takes notice of a private man, and
therefore with him 'tis more secret, and the crime's the
less when 'tis not known.   405
LADY FIDGET
You say true. I'faith, I think you are in the right on't.
'Tis not an injury to a husband till it be an injury to our
honours; so that a woman of honour loses no honour
with a private person; and to say truth –
DAINTY (*Apart to* SQUEAMISH)
So, the little fellow is grown a private person – with her.   410
LADY FIDGET
But still my dear, dear honour.

Enter SIR JASPAR, HORNER, DORILANT

SIR JASPAR
Ay, my dear, dear of honour, thou hast still so much

399 *ramble* allow our lascivious thoughts to wander. John D. Patterson, 'The
    Restoration *Ramble*', *Notes and Queries* vol. 226 (1981), 209–10, notes
    that at this time the verb often meant 'go out in search of sex', quoting
    Wycherley's *Love in a Wood* among other sources.
400 *in your discourse,* i.e., in your discourse at least
403 *private* without rank in society
404–5 *the crime's the less when 'tis not known* a libertine commonplace; 'To be
    taken, to be seen, / These have crimes accounted been' (Jonson, *Volpone*
    III.vii.181–2)
412 *dear of honour* dear to me because of your virtue

honour in thy mouth –
HORNER (*Aside*)
    That she has none elsewhere.
LADY FIDGET
    Oh, what d'ye mean to bring in these upon us?   415
DAINTY
    Foh! these are as bad as wits.
SQUEAMISH
    Foh!
LADY FIDGET
    Let us leave the room.
SIR JASPAR
    Stay, stay; faith, to tell you the naked truth –
LADY FIDGET
    Fie, Sir Jaspar, do not use that word 'naked'.   420
SIR JASPAR
    Well, well, in short, I have business at Whitehall, and
    cannot go to the play with you, therefore would have
    you go –
LADY FIDGET
    With those two to a play?
SIR JASPAR
    No, not with t'other but with Master Horner.   There 425
    can be no more scandal to go with him than with Master
    Tattle, or Master Limberham.
LADY FIDGET
    With that nasty fellow! No – no!
SIR JASPAR
    Nay, prithee dear, hear me.   *Whispers to* LADY FIDGET
HORNER
    Ladies –   430
    HORNER, DORILANT *drawing near* SQUEAMISH *and* DAINTY
DAINTY
    Stand off!

416   *as bad as wits* who were notorious for ribaldry and debauchery
421   *Whitehall* i.e., at court. See I.i. 115–16 and introduction, p. xiv.
426–7 *Master Tattle, or Master Limberham* names probably of the 'two old
      civil gentlemen' mentioned at II.i.496, *Tattle* suggesting idle talk,
      Limberham obsequiousness.   Wycherley apparently invented the
      name Limberham, borrowed by Dryden for a 'tame, foolish keeper'
      in *The Kind Keeper; or, Mr Limberham* (1678). Tattle was used by
      Congreve for a fop in *Love for Love* (1695).
429   sd Sir Jaspar has already told his wife Horner is a eunuch (I.i.109),
      but the context suggests that is what he whispers about here.   The
      effect is to leave centre stage for the comic exchange between the
      wits and the other ladies.

SQUEAMISH

Do not approach us!

DAINTY

You herd with the wits, you are obscenity all over.

SQUEAMISH

And I would as soon look upon a picture of Adam and
Eve, without fig leaves, as any of you, if I could help it, 435
therefore keep off, and do not make us sick.

DORILANT

What a devil are these?

HORNER

Why, these are pretenders to honour, as critics to wit,
only by censuring others; and as every raw, peevish,
out-of-humoured, affected, dull, tea-drinking, arith- 440
metical fop sets up for a wit, by railing at men of sense,
so these for honour by railing at the court and ladies of
as great honour as quality.

SIR JASPAR

Come, Master Horner, I must desire you to go with
these ladies to the play, sir. 445

HORNER

I, sir?

SIR JASPAR

Ay, ay, come, sir.

HORNER

I must beg your pardon, sir, and theirs. I will not be
seen in women's company in public again for the world.

SIR JASPAR

Ha, ha! strange aversion! 450

SQUEAMISH

No, he's for women's company in private.

SIR JASPAR

He – poor man – he! ha, ha, ha!

DAINTY

'Tis a greater shame amongst lewd fellows to be seen in
virtuous women's company than for the women to be
seen with them. 455

HORNER

Indeed, madam, the time was I only hated virtuous
women, but now I hate the other too; I beg your
pardon, ladies.

---

437 *What a devil* what the devil
441 *arithmetical* excessively precise; not recorded in this sense in *OED*

LADY FIDGET

You are very obliging, sir, because we would not be
troubled with you.   460

SIR JASPAR

In sober sadness, he shall go.

DORILANT

Nay, if he won't, I am ready to wait upon the ladies;
and I think I am the fitter man.

SIR JASPAR

You, sir? No, I thank you for that. Master Horner is a
privileged man amongst the virtuous ladies; 'twill be a 465
great while before you are so, he, he, he! He's my wife's
gallant, he, he, he! No, pray withdraw, sir, for as I take
it, the virtuous ladies have no business with you.

DORILANT

And I am sure he can have none with them. 'Tis strange
a man can't come amongst virtuous women now, but 470
upon the same terms as men are admitted into the great
Turk's seraglio; but heavens keep me from being an
ombre player with 'em! But where is Pinchwife?

Exit DORILANT

SIR JASPAR

Come, come, man; what, avoid the sweet society of
woman-kind? – that sweet, soft, gentle, tame, noble 475
creature, woman, made for man's companion –

HORNER

So is that soft, gentle, tame, and more noble creature a
spaniel, and has all their tricks; can fawn, lie down,
suffer beating, and fawn the more; barks at your friends
when they come to see you; makes your bed hard; gives 480
you fleas, and the mange sometimes. And all the
difference is, the spaniel's the more faithful animal and
fawns but upon one master.

SIR JASPAR

He, he, he!

---

461 *in sober sadness* in all seriousness; perhaps an old-fashioned asseveration
471–2 *great Turk* Sultan of Turkey; mentioned again at IV.iii.358
473 *ombre* card game said to have made fashionable by Charles II's wife
     Catherine of Braganza. From the Spanish *juego del hombre*, the man's
     game. So Dorilant is saying both that he does not want to play cards
     with the ladies and that he does not want to play at being a man with
     them. See similar pun at IV.iii.215–17.

SQUEAMISH

Oh, the rude beast!   485

DAINTY

Insolent brute!

LADY FIDGET

Brute!   Stinking, mortified, rotten French wether, to
dare –

SIR JASPAR

Hold, an't please your ladyship. – For shame, Master
Horner, your mother was a woman. – (*Aside*) Now shall   490
I never reconcile 'em. – Hark you, madam, take my
advice in your anger. You know you often want one to
make up your drolling pack of ombre players; and you
may cheat him easily, for he's an ill gamester, and
consequently loves play. Besides, you know, you have   495
but two old civil gentlemen (with stinking breaths too)
to wait upon you abroad; take in the third into your
service. The other are but crazy; and a lady should
have   a   supernumerary   gentleman-usher,   as   a
supernumerary coachhorse, lest sometimes you should   500
be forced to stay at home.

LADY FIDGET

But are you sure he loves play, and has money?

SIR JASPAR

He loves play as much as you, and has money as much
as I.

LADY FIDGET

Then I am contented to make him pay for his scurrility;   505
money makes up in a measure all other wants in men. –
(*Aside*) Those whom we cannot make hold for gallants,
we make fine.

487 *mortified, rotten French wether* literally, tenderised but rotten meat of a
       castrated ram;   *OED* 5 quoting Fynes Moryson, *An Itinerary* (1617),
       'The French alone delight in mortified meats' (III.134); metaphorically,
       man made impotent by the pox
493 *drolling* ridiculous
494 *gamester* gambler
495 *play* gambling
498 *but crazy* almost ga-ga
499 *gentleman usher* attendant on a person of rank. They were going out of
       fashion, as Etherege suggests: *The Man of Mode* (1676) I.i.67–9.
       as as she would have
507 *make hold for* occupy the position of
508 *make fine* require to pay. But as a *fine* was often a payment to avoid the
       duties of office, there is probably a satirical reference to Horner's
       presumed impotence.

SIR JASPAR (*Aside*)

So, so; now to mollify, to wheedle him. – Master
Horner, will you never keep civil company? Methinks 510
'tis time now, since you are only fit for them. Come,
come, man, you must e'en fall to visiting our wives,
eating at our tables, drinking tea with our virtuous
relations after dinner, dealing cards to 'em, reading plays
and gazettes to 'em, picking fleas out of their shocks for 515
'em, collecting receipts, new songs, women, pages, and
footmen for 'em.

HORNER

I hope they'll afford me better employment, sir.

SIR JASPAR

He, he, he! 'Tis fit you know your work before you
come into your place; and since you are unprovided of a 520
lady to flatter, and a good house to eat at, pray frequent
mine, and call my wife mistress, and she shall call you
gallant, according to the custom.

HORNER

Who, I?

SIR JASPAR

Faith, thou shalt for my sake; come, for my sake only.   525

HORNER

For your sake –

SIR JASPAR

Come, come, here's a gamester for you; let him be a
little familiar sometimes; nay, what if a little rude?
Gamesters may be rude with ladies, you know.

LADY FIDGET

Yes, losing gamesters have a privilege with women.   530

---

509 *wheedle* win over. See also l. 541.
513 *drinking tea* harmless custom especially hateful to Horner. See l. 440.
515 *gazettes* newspapers
     shocks poodles
516 *receipts* recipes
     women waiting women
522–3 The custom is observed by Lady Fidget and Horner, ll.604–5 (and by
     the somewhat similarly related Lucy and Gripe, *Love in a Wood*
     V.i.151–2). The words *mistress* and *gallant* could be more or less
     innocent; Friedman quotes Thomas Blount, *Glossographia* (1670):
     'Gallant ... Servant or Platonick to a Lady' (p. 287).
527 *gamester* gambler, as at l. 494. But the slang sense, 'wencher', could
     also be intended.

HORNER

I always thought the contrary, that the winning gamester
had most privilege with women; for when you have lost
your money to a man, you'll lose anything you have, all
you have, they say, and he may use you as he pleases.

SIR JASPAR

He, he, he! Well, win or lose, you shall have your liberty 535
with her.

LADY FIDGET

As he behaves himself; and for your sake I'll give him
admittance and freedom.

HORNER

All sorts of freedom, madam?

SIR JASPAR

Ay, ay, ay, all sorts of freedom thou canst take, and so go 540
to her, begin thy new employment, wheedle her, jest
with her, and be better acquainted one with another.

HORNER (*Aside*)

I think I know her already, therefore may venture with
her, my secret for hers.

                         HORNER *and* LADY FIDGET *whisper*

SIR JASPAR

Sister, cuz, I have provided an innocent playfellow for 545
you there.

DAINTY

Who, he?

SQUEAMISH

There's a playfellow indeed!

SIR JASPAR

Yes, sure, what, he is good enough to play at cards, blind
man's buff, or the fool with sometimes.   550

SQUEAMISH

Foh! we'll have no such playfellows.

DAINTY

No, sir, you shan't choose playfellows for us, we thank
you.

543   *venture* Q2–5, O (venter Q1, probably just alternative spelling), bargain
545   *cuz* abbreviation of cousin, used in familiar address, especially to
      relatives
548   *playfellow* sexual partner; *double entendre.* See Farmer and Henley under
      'play' and Partridge, *Shakespeare's Bawdy* (1968), p.162.

SIR JASPAR

    Nay, pray hear me.   *Whispering to them*

LADY FIDGET

    But, poor gentleman, could you be so generous, so truly 555
a man of honour, as for the sakes of us women of
honour, to cause yourself to be reported no man? No
man! And to suffer yourself the greatest shame that
could fall upon a man, that none might fall upon us
women by your conversation?   But indeed, sir, as 560
perfectly, perfectly, the same man as before your going
into France, sir? As perfectly, perfectly, sir?

HORNER

    As perfectly, perfectly, madam. Nay, I scorn you should
take my word;   I desire to be tried only, madam.

LADY FIDGET

    Well, that's spoken again like a man of honour; all men 565
of honour desire to come to the test.   But, indeed,
generally, you men report such things of yourselves, one
does not know how or whom to believe; and it is come
to that pass, we dare not take your words no more than
your tailors, without some staid servant of yours be 570
bound with you. But I have so strong a faith in your
honour, dear, dear, noble sir, that I'd forfeit mine for
yours at any time, dear sir.

HORNER

    No, madam, you should not need to forfeit it for me. I
have given you security already to save you harmless, my 575
late reputation being so well known in the world,
madam.

LADY FIDGET

    But if upon any future falling out, or upon a suspicion of
my taking the trust out of your hands, to employ some
other, you yourself should betray your trust, dear sir? I 580
mean, if you'll give me leave to speak obscenely, you

---

554 sd Presumably he tells them Horner is a eunuch, while Horner assures
      Lady Fidget he is not.
560 *conversation* intercourse; *double entendre*
569–70 *no more than your tailors* any more than your tailors would
570 *staid* settled in character
      be bound literally, stand surety for payment (to the tailor); metaphorically
      perhaps, give sexual satisfaction (if the gallant does not)
575 *save you harmless* save you from harm (by scandal)
581 *obscenely* Characteristically, she associates plain dealing with
      indecency.

might tell, dear sir.

HORNER

If I did, nobody would believe me; the reputation of
impotency is as hardly recovered again in the world as
that of cowardice, dear madam.   585

LADY FIDGET

Nay, then, as one may say, you may do your worst, dear,
dear, sir.

SIR JASPAR

Come, is your ladyship reconciled to him yet? Have you
agreed on matters? For I must be gone to Whitehall.

LADY FIDGET

Why, indeed, Sir Jaspar, Master Horner is a thousand, 590
thousand times a better man than I thought him.
Cousin Squeamish, Sister Dainty, I can name him now,
truly; not long ago, you know, I thought his very name
obscenity, and I would as soon have lain with him as
have named him.   595

SIR JASPAR

Very likely, poor madam.

DAINTY

I believe it.

SQUEAMISH

No doubt on't.

SIR JASPAR

Well, well, that your ladyship is as virtuous as any she, I
know, and him all the town knows, he, he, he! 600
Therefore, now you like him, get you gone to your
business together; go, go, to your business, I say,
pleasure, whilst I go to my pleasure, business.

LADY FIDGET

Come then, dear gallant.

HORNER

Come away, my dearest mistress.   605

SIR JASPAR

So, so; why 'tis as I'd have it.

Exit SIR JASPAR

---

584   *recovered again* recovered from
602   *business* both frivolous activity and sexual intercourse. Sir Jaspar
      intends the first irony, but not the second. Lady Fidget makes the
      bawdy meaning quite clear in l. 609 below.
606   It is as Sir Jaspar would have it partly because Lady Fidget and Horner
      are using the terms he suggested (ll. 522–3) – but not in the senses he
      intended.

HORNER

And as I'd have it.

LADY FIDGET

Who for his business, from his wife will run,

Takes the best care, to have her business done.

Exeunt omnes

Act III, Scene i

ALITHEA *and* MRS PINCHWIFE

ALITHEA

Sister, what ails you? You are grown melancholy.

MRS PINCHWIFE

Would it not make anyone melancholy, to see you go
every day fluttering about abroad, whilst I must stay at
home like a poor lonely sullen bird in a cage?

ALITHEA

Ay, sister, but you came young and just from the nest to   5
your cage, so that I thought you liked it; and could be
as cheerful in't as others that took their flight themselves
early, and are hopping abroad in the open air.

MRS PINCHWIFE

Nay, I confess I was quiet enough till my husband told
me what pure lives the London ladies live abroad, with   10
their dancing, meetings, and junketings, and dressed
every day in their best gowns; and I warrant you, play
at ninepins every day of the week, so they do.

Enter PINCHWIFE

PINCHWIFE

Come, what's here to do? You are putting the town
pleasures in her head, and setting her a-longing.   15

ALITHEA

Yes, after ninepins! You suffer none to give her those
longings you mean, but yourself.

PINCHWIFE

I tell her of the vanities of the town like a confessor.

---

10 *pure* wonderful; childish or vulgar term
13 *ninepins* a game 'still kept in action by the bumpkins', according to
    Francis Kirkman, *The Unlucky Citizen* (1673), p.10; unlikely to have
    been played by the London ladies

ALITHEA

A confessor! Just such a confessor as he that, by
forbidding a silly ostler to grease the horse's teeth, 20
taught him to do't.

PINCHWIFE

Come, Mistress Flippant, good precepts are lost when
bad examples are still before us. The liberty you take
abroad makes her hanker after it, and out of humour at
home. Poor wretch! she desired not to come to 25
London; I would bring her.

ALITHEA

Very well.

PINCHWIFE

She has been this week in town, and never desired, till
this afternoon, to go abroad.

ALITHEA

Was she not at a play yesterday?   30

PINCHWIFE

Yes, but she ne'er asked me. I was myself the cause of
her going.

ALITHEA

Then, if she ask you again, you are the cause of her
asking, and not my example.

PINCHWIFE

Well, tomorrow night I shall be rid of you; and the next 35
day, before 'tis light, she and I'll be rid of the town, and
my dreadful apprehensions. Come, be not melancholy,
for thou shalt go into the country after tomorrow,
dearest.

ALITHEA

Great comfort!   40

MRS PINCHWIFE

Pish! what d'ye tell me of the country for?

PINCHWIFE

How's this? What, pish at the country?

MRS PINCHWIFE

Let me alone, I am not well.

PINCHWIFE

O, if that be all – what ails my dearest?

20–1 Sophisticated ostlers used grease to inhibit feeding, and so make a
better profit on the provender.

22 *Mistress Flippant* Lady Flippant was a hypocritical character in *Love
in a Wood;* the word means 'impertinently voluble' (*OED* 2.b).

MRS PINCHWIFE

Truly I don't know; but I have not been well since you   45
told me there was a gallant at the play in love with me.

PINCHWIFE

Ha!

ALITHEA

That's by my example, too!

PINCHWIFE

Nay, if you are not well, but are so concerned because a
lewd fellow chanced to lie and say he liked you, you'll   50
make me sick too.

MRS PINCHWIFE

Of what sickness?

PINCHWIFE

O, of that which is worse than the plague – jealousy.

MRS PINCHWIFE

Pish, you jeer! I'm sure there's no such disease in our
receipt-book at home.   55

PINCHWIFE

No, thou never met'st with it, poor innocent. (*Aside*)
Well, if thou cuckold me, 'twill be my own fault, for
cuckolds and bastards are generally makers of their own
fortune.

MRS PINCHWIFE

Well, but pray, bud, let's go to a play tonight.   60

PINCHWIFE

'Tis just done, she comes from it; but why are you so
eager to see a play?

MRS PINCHWIFE

Faith, dear, not that I care one pin for their talk there,
but I like to look upon the player-men, and would see, if
I could, the gallant you say loves me; that's all, dear   65
bud.

PINCHWIFE

Is that all, dear bud?

ALITHEA

This proceeds from my example.

---

54 *you jeer* you are joking; expression frequently used by Mrs Pinchwife
57–9 'The wary fool is by his care betrayed, / As cuckolds by their jealousy
    are made' (*The Gentleman Dancing-Master* III.i.595–6)
61 *'Tis just done* i.e., it is early evening, as plays were performed in the
    late afternoon

MRS PINCHWIFE

But if the play be done, let's go abroad, however, dear
bud. 70

PINCHWIFE

Come, have a little patience, and thou shalt go into the
country on Friday.

MRS PINCHWIFE

Therefore I would see first some sights, to tell my
neighbours of. Nay, I will go abroad, that's once.

ALITHEA

I'm the cause of this desire too. 75

PINCHWIFE

But now I think on't, who was the cause of Horner's
coming to my lodging today? That was you.

ALITHEA

No, you, because you would not let him see your
handsome wife out of your lodging.

MRS PINCHWIFE

Why, O Lord! Did the gentleman come hither to see me 80
indeed?

PINCHWIFE

No, no. – You are not cause of that damned question
too, Mistress Alithea? (*Aside*) Well, she's in the right of
it. He is in love with my wife – and comes after her – 'tis
so – but I'll nip his love in the bud; lest he should follow 85
us into the country and break his chariot-wheel near our
house on purpose for an excuse to come to't. But I
think I know the town.

MRS PINCHWIFE

Come, pray bud, let's go abroad before 'tis late. For I
will go, that's flat and plain. 90

PINCHWIFE (*Aside*)

So! the obstinacy already of a town-wife, and I must,
whilst she's here, humour her like one. – Sister, how
shall we do, that she may not be seen or known?

ALITHEA

Let her put on her mask.

PINCHWIFE

Pshaw! A mask makes people but the more inquisitive, 95
and is as ridiculous a disguise as a stage beard; her
shape, stature, habit will be known. And if we should
meet with   Horner,   he   would   be   sure   to   take

---

74 *that's once* that's flat; vulgarism
86 *chariot* carriage

acquaintance with us, must wish her joy, kiss her, talk to
her, leer upon her, and the devil and all. No, I'll not use 100
her to a mask, 'tis dangerous; for masks have made more
cuckolds than the best faces that ever were known.

ALITHEA

How will you do then?

MRS PINCHWIFE

Nay, shall we go? The Exchange will be shut, and I
have a mind to see that.   105

PINCHWIFE

So – I have it – I'll dress her up in the suit we are to
carry down to her brother, little Sir James;   nay, I
understand the town tricks. Come, let's go dress her. A
mask! No; a woman masked, like a covered dish, gives
a man curiosity and appetite, when, it may be, 110
uncovered, 'twould turn his stomach; no, no.

ALITHEA

Indeed your comparison is something a greasy one. But
I had a gentle gallant used to say, 'A beauty masked, like
the sun in eclipse, gathers together more gazers than if it
shined out'.   115

Exeunt

[Act III, Scene ii]

The scene changes to the New Exchange
[CLASP *and other shopkeepers*]
Enter HORNER, HARCOURT, DORILANT

DORILANT

Engaged to women, and not sup with us?

HORNER

Ay, a pox on 'em all.

HARCOURT

You were much a more reasonable man in the morning,
and had as noble resolutions against 'em as a widower of
a week's liberty.   5

100 *use* accustom
104 *The Exchange* See II.i.4 and note.
107 *little Sir James* Mrs Pinchwife's brother would have to be small, or the
      suit would not fit Mrs Boutell, who played the part in 1675. The name
      also suggests that his family are country gentry.
112 *greasy* distasteful; with a quibble on the literal sense
113 *like* Q2–5, O (lik'd Q1)

DORILANT

Did I ever think to see you keep company with women in vain?

HORNER [*Aside*]

In vain! No – 'tis, since I can't love 'em, to be revenged on 'em.

HARCOURT

Now your sting is gone, you looked in the box, amongst   10
all those women, like a drone in the hive, all upon you; shoved and ill-used by 'em all, and thrust from one side to t'other.

DORILANT

Yet he must be buzzing amongst 'em still, like other old beetle-headed, lickerish drones. Avoid 'em, and hate   15
'em as they hate you.

HORNER

Because I do hate 'em and would hate 'em yet more, I'll frequent 'em. You may see by marriage, nothing makes a man hate a woman more, than her constant conversation. In short, I converse with 'em, as you do with   20
rich fools, to laugh at 'em and use 'em ill.

DORILANT

But I would no more sup with women, unless I could lie with 'em, than sup with a rich coxcomb, unless I could cheat him.

HORNER

Yes, I have known thee sup with a fool for his drinking;   25
if he could set out your hand that way only, you were satisfied, and if he were a wine-swallowing mouth 'twas enough.

HARCOURT

Yes, a man drinks often with a fool, as he tosses with a marker, only to keep his hand in ure. But do the ladies   30
drink?

---

10 *box* i.e., at the theatre

15 *beetle-headed* stupid
     lickerish greedy, lustful

20 *conversation* intercourse. See I.i.217.

26 *set out your hand* serve your purpose. Horner perhaps refers to getting free drink, though Harcourt takes him to mean Dorilant will drink with a fool just to keep in practice.

29–30 *tosses with a marker, only to keep his hand in ure* throws dice with a scorer, just to keep in practice (*OED* Ure *sb.*[1] I.1.a)

HORNER

Yes, sir, and I shall have the pleasure at least of laying
'em flat with a bottle, and bring as much scandal that
way upon 'em as formerly t'other.

HARCOURT

Perhaps you may prove as weak a brother amongst 'em   35
that way as t'other.

DORILANT

Foh! drinking with women is as unnatural as scolding
with 'em. But 'tis a pleasure of decayed fornicators, and
the basest way of quenching love.

HARCOURT

Nay, 'tis drowning love instead of quenching it. But   40
leave us for civil women too!

DORILANT

Ay, when he can't be the better for 'em. We hardly
pardon a man that leaves his friend for a wench, and
that's a pretty lawful call.

HORNER

Faith, I would not leave you for 'em, if they would not   45
drink.

DORILANT

Who would disappoint his company at Lewis's, for a
gossiping?

HARCOURT

Foh! Wine and women, good apart, together as
nauseous as sack and sugar. But hark you, sir, before   50
you go, a little of your advice; an old maimed general,
when unfit for action, is fittest for counsel. I have other
designs upon women than eating and drinking with
them. I am in love with Sparkish's mistress, whom he is
to marry tomorrow. Now how shall I get her?   55

Enter SPARKISH, *looking about*

HORNER

Why, here comes one will help you to her.

---

35 *brother* member of their fraternity. Harcourt seems to know they are
     great drinkers.
37–8 *scolding with 'em* joining them in abusive gossip
41 *civil* well-bred
47 *Lewis's* presumably a tavern
50 *sack* Spanish wine, customarily served with sugar. Harcourt's taste is in
     advance of his time.

HARCOURT

He! He, I tell you, is my rival, and will hinder my love.

HORNER

No, a foolish rival and a jealous husband assist their
rival's designs; for they are sure to make their women
hate them, which is the first step to their love for another   60
man.

HARCOURT

But I cannot come near his mistress but in his company.

HORNER

Still the better for you, for fools are most easily cheated
when they themselves are accessories; and he is to be
bubbled of his mistress, as of his money, the common   65
mistress, by keeping him company.

SPARKISH

Who is that, that is to be bubbled? Faith, let me snack, I
ha'n't met with a bubble since Christmas. Gad, I think
bubbles are like their brother woodcocks, go out with
the cold weather.   70

HARCOURT (*Apart to* HORNER)

A pox! he did not hear all I hope.

SPARKISH

Come, you bubbling rogues you, where do we sup? –
Oh, Harcourt, my mistress tells me you have been
making fierce love to her all the play long, ha, ha! – But
I –   75

HARCOURT

I make love to her?

SPARKISH

Nay, I forgive thee; for I think I know thee, and I know
her, but I am sure I know myself.

HARCOURT

Did she tell you so? I see all women are like these of the
Exchange, who, to enhance the price of their   80
commodities, report to their fond customers offers
which were never made 'em.

HORNER

Ay, women are as apt to tell before the intrigue as men

65 *bubbled* tricked
67 *snack* share
70 *woodcocks* dupes. Woodcock is the name of a fop in Shadwell's *The
Sullen Lovers* (1668).
go out disappear
81 *fond* foolish, credulous

after it, and so show themselves the vainer sex. But hast
thou a mistress, Sparkish? 'Tis as hard for me to believe   85
it as that thou ever hadst a bubble, as you bragged just
now.

SPARKISH

Oh, your servant, sir; are you at your raillery, sir? But
we were some of us beforehand with you today at the
play. The wits were something bold with you, sir; did   90
you not hear us laugh?

HARCOURT

Yes, but I thought you had gone to plays to laugh at the
poet's wit, not at your own.

SPARKISH

Your servant, sir; no, I thank you. Gad, I go to a play as
to a country treat. I carry my own wine to one, and my   95
own wit to t'other, or else I'm sure I should not be merry
at either. And the reason why we are so often louder
than the players is because we think we speak more wit,
and so become the poet's rivals in his audience. For to
tell you the truth, we hate the silly rogues; nay, so much 100
that we find fault even with their bawdy upon the stage,
whilst we talk nothing else in the pit as loud.

HORNER

But, why should'st thou hate the silly poets? Thou hast
too much wit to be one, and they, like whores, are only
hated by each other. And thou dost scorn writing, I'm   105
sure.

SPARKISH

Yes, I'd have you to know, I scorn writing. But women,
women, that make men do all foolish things, make 'em
write songs too. Everybody does it. 'Tis even as
common with lovers as playing with fans; and you can   110
no more help rhyming to your Phyllis than drinking to
your Phyllis.

HARCOURT

Nay, poetry in love is no more to be avoided than
jealousy.

---

88 *your servant* here, a polite form of disagreement
92 sp HARCOURT *Har.* Q1-5, O, but perhaps *Hor.* intended, as Sparkish's
    speech is addressed to Horner. However, perhaps Harcourt defends him.
111 Poets who wrote songs about Phyllis included Rochester, Sedley, and
    Wycherley himself. Dorset's 'A Song on Black Bess' (1668) begins:
    'Methinks the poor town has been troubled too long / With Phyllis and
    Chloris in every song' (*Poems*, ed. Brice Harris, p. 91).

DORILANT

But the poets damned your songs, did they?   115

SPARKISH

Damn the poets! They turned 'em into burlesque, as
they call it. That burlesque is a hocus-pocus trick they
have got, which by the virtue of hictius doctius, topsy-
turvy, they make a wise and witty man in the world a
fool upon the stage, you know not how. – And 'tis 120
therefore I hate 'em too, for I know not but it may be my
own case; for they'll put a man into a play for looking
asquint. Their predecessors were contented to make
serving-men only their stage-fools, but these rogues
must have gentlemen, with a pox to 'em, nay knights. 125
And indeed you shall hardly see a fool upon the stage
but he's a knight. And to tell you the truth, they have
kept me these six years from being a knight in earnest,
for fear of being knighted in a play, and dubbed a fool.

DORILANT

Blame 'em not, they must follow their copy, the age.   130

HARCOURT

But why should'st thou be afraid of being in a play, who
expose yourself every day in the playhouses, and as
public places?

HORNER

'Tis but being on the stage, instead of standing on a
bench in the pit.   135

DORILANT

Don't you give money to painters to draw you like? And
are you afraid of your pictures at length in a playhouse,
where all your mistresses may see you?

SPARKISH

A pox! Painters don't draw the smallpox or pimples in
one's face. Come, damn all your silly authors whatever, 140
all books and booksellers, by the world, and all readers,
courteous or uncourteous.

---

118 *hictius doctius* nonsense term used by jugglers
125 *knights* like Sir Martin Mar-all (see I.i.259 note), Etherege's Sir Oliver
     Cockwood (*She Would if she Could*, 1668), Wycherley's own Sir Simon
     Addleplot (*Love in a Wood*), and many more
132 *as* equally
136 *like* accurately
137 *at length* at full length
142 *courteous* term formerly used by authors in addressing their readers

HARCOURT

But, who comes here, Sparkish?

Enter PINCHWIFE *and his wife in man's clothes,*
ALITHEA, LUCY *her maid*

SPARKISH

Oh hide me! There's my mistress too.

SPARKISH *hides himself behind* HARCOURT

HARCOURT

She sees you.   145

SPARKISH

But I will not see her. 'Tis time to go to Whitehall, and
I must not fail the drawing-room.

HARCOURT

Pray, first carry me, and reconcile me to her.

SPARKISH

Another time! Faith, the King will have supped.

HARCOURT

Not with the worse stomach for thy absence! Thou art   150
one of those fools that think their attendance at the
King's meals as necessary as his physicians', when you
are more troublesome to him than his doctors, or his
dogs.

SPARKISH

Pshaw! I know my interest, sir. Prithee, hide me.   155

HORNER

Your servant, Pinchwife. – What, he knows us not!

PINCHWIFE (*To his wife, aside*)

Come along.

MRS PINCHWIFE

Pray, have you any ballads? Give me sixpenny worth.

---

147 *fail* fail to attend
149 *the King will have supped* 'All persons who had been properly introduced
      might, without special invitation, go to see [Charles II] dine, sup, dance,
      and play at hazard' (Macaulay, *History of England,* ed. C.H. Firth, vol.1,
      p. 358).
152–4 Charles II 'had not more application to anything, than the preservation
      of his health' (Halifax, *Complete Works,* ed. J.P. Kenyon, p. 264). He
      also 'took delight to have a number of little spaniels follow him, and lie
      in his bed-chamber, where often-times he suffered the bitches to puppy
      and give suck, which rendered it very offensive, and indeed made the
      whole Court nasty and stinking' (Evelyn, *Diary,* 6 February 1685).

CLASP

We have no ballads.

MRS PINCHWIFE

Then give me *Covent Garden Drollery* and a play or two. 160
– Oh, here's *Tarugo's Wiles* and *The Slighted Maiden*. I'll
have them.

PINCHWIFE (*Apart to her*)

No, plays are not for your reading. Come along; will
you discover yourself?

HORNER

Who is that pretty youth with him, Sparkish?   165

SPARKISH

I believe his wife's brother, because he's something like
her; but I never saw her but once.

HORNER

Extremely handsome. I have seen a face like it too. Let
us follow 'em.

> *Exeunt* PINCHWIFE, MRS PINCHWIFE;
> ALITHEA, LUCY, HORNER, DORILANT *following them*

HARCOURT

Come, Sparkish, your mistress saw you, and will be 170
angry you go not to her. Besides I would fain be
reconciled to her, which none but you can do, dear
friend.

SPARKISH

Well, that's a better reason, dear friend. I would not go
near her now, for hers or my own sake, but I can deny 175
you nothing; for though I have known thee a great
while, never go, if I do not love thee as well as a new
acquaintance.

HARCOURT

I am obliged to you indeed, dear friend. I would be well
with her, only to be well with thee still; for these ties to 180
wives usually dissolve all ties to friends. I would be
contented she should enjoy you a-nights, but I would

---

159 sp *CLASP* not mentioned in the list of 'The Persons'. Friedman suggests
the name is an abbreviation of 'clasp-man', which could have meant a
bookseller (*OED* Clasp *sb.* 7).

160 *Covent Garden Drollery* compilation by Alexander Brome of songs,
prologues and epilogues from plays, published 1672

161 *Tarugo's Wiles* comedy by Sir Thomas St Serfe, 1668; *The Slighted
Maiden* comedy by Sir Robert Stapleton, 1663. Mrs Pinchwife does not
know these plays are completely unfashionable.

177 *never go* don't worry. *Never stir* (ll. 184–5) means much the same.

have you to myself a-days, as I have had, dear friend.
SPARKISH

And thou shalt enjoy me a-days, dear, dear friend, never
stir;   and I'll be divorced from her, sooner than from 185
thee. Come along –
HARCOURT (*Aside*)

So we are hard put to't, when we make our rival our
procurer;   but neither she nor her brother would let me
come near her now. When all's done, a rival is the best
cloak to steal to a mistress under, without suspicion; 190
and when we have once got to her as we desire, we
throw him off like other cloaks.

Exit SPARKISH, *and* HARCOURT *following him*

Re-enter PINCHWIFE, MRS PINCHWIFE *in man's clothes*

PINCHWIFE (*To* ALITHEA [*off-stage*])

Sister, if you will not go, we must leave you.   (*Aside*)
The fool her gallant and she will muster up all the young
saunterers of this place, and they will leave their dear 195
seamstresses to follow us. What a swarm of cuckolds
and cuckold-makers are here!   – Come, let's be gone,
Mistress Margery.
MRS PINCHWIFE

Don't you believe that, I ha'n't half my bellyfull of sights
yet.   200
PINCHWIFE

Then walk this way.
MRS PINCHWIFE

Lord, what a power of brave signs are here! Stay – the
Bull's Head, the Ram's Head, and the Stag's Head!
Dear –
PINCHWIFE

Nay, if every husband's proper sign here were visible, 205
they would be all alike.
MRS PINCHWIFE

What d'ye mean by that, bud?
PINCHWIFE

'Tis no matter – no matter, bud.

195–6 There were many seamstresses' shops in the New Exchange. Jokes
      about seamstresses and male customers were as common as those about
      secretaries and businessmen today.
202 *signs* tradesmen's signs or symbols. See I.i.299.
205 *husband's proper sign* cuckold's horns. Pinchwife is painfully aware that
      all the signs show horned creatures.

MRS PINCHWIFE
Pray tell me; nay, I will know.
PINCHWIFE
They would be all bulls', stags', and rams' heads.   210
Exeunt PINCHWIFE, MRS PINCHWIFE

Re-enter SPARKISH, HARCOURT, ALITHEA, LUCY
at t'other door

SPARKISH
Come, dear madam, for my sake you shall be reconciled
to him.
ALITHEA
For your sake I hate him.
HARCOURT
That's something too cruel, madam, to hate me for his
sake.   215
SPARKISH
Ay indeed, madam, too, too cruel to me, to hate my
friend for my sake.
ALITHEA
I hate him because he is your enemy; and you ought to
hate him too, for making love to me, if you love me.
SPARKISH
That's a good one; I, hate a man for loving you! If he   220
did love you, 'tis but what he can't help; and 'tis your
fault not his if he admires you. I, hate a man for being
of my opinion? I'll ne'er do it, by the world.
ALITHEA
Is it for your honour or mine, to suffer a man to make
love to me, who am to marry you tomorrow?   225
SPARKISH
Is it for your honour or mine, to have me jealous? That
he makes love to you is a sign you are handsome; and
that I am not jealous is a sign you are virtuous. That, I
think, is for your honour.
ALITHEA
But 'tis your honour too I am concerned for.   230
HARCOURT
But why, dearest madam, will you be more concerned
for his honour than he is himself? Let his honour alone,
for my sake and his. He, he has no honour –

---

210 sd *at t'other door* i.e., on the same side of the stage. See Introduction,
     p. xxvii.

SPARKISH

How's that?

HARCOURT

But what my dear friend can guard himself.   235

SPARKISH

Oho, that's right again.

HARCOURT

Your care of his honour argues his neglect of it, which is
no honour to my dear friend here; therefore once more,
let his honour go which way it will, dear madam.

SPARKISH

Ay, ay, were it for my honour to marry a woman whose 240
virtue I suspected, and could not trust her in a friend's
hands?

ALITHEA

Are you not afraid to lose me?

HARCOURT

He afraid to lose you, madam! No, no – you may see
how the most estimable and most glorious creature in 245
the world is valued by him. Will you not see it?

SPARKISH

Right, honest Frank, I have that noble value for her that
I cannot be jealous of her.

ALITHEA

You mistake him. He means you care not for me nor
who has me.   250

SPARKISH

Lord, madam, I see you are jealous! Will you wrest a
poor man's meaning from his words?

ALITHEA

You astonish me, sir, with your want of jealousy.

SPARKISH

And you make me giddy, madam, with your jealousy
and fears, and virtue and honour. Gad, I see virtue 255
makes a woman as troublesome as a little reading or
learning.

ALITHEA

Monstrous!

LUCY (*Behind*)

Well, to see what easy husbands these women of quality
can meet with! A poor chambermaid can never have 260
such lady-like luck. Besides, he's thrown away upon

251 *jealous* impassioned, apprehensive
259 *easy* complaisant

her; she'll make no use of her fortune, her blessing;
none to a gentleman for a pure cuckold, for it requires
good breeding to be a cuckold.

ALITHEA

I tell you then plainly, he pursues me to marry me.   265

SPARKISH

Pshaw!

HARCOURT

Come, madam, you see you strive in vain to make him
jealous of me. My dear friend is the kindest creature in
the world to me.

SPARKISH

Poor fellow.   270

HARCOURT

But his kindness only is not enough for me, without
your favour. Your good opinion, dear madam, 'tis that
must perfect my happiness.   Good gentleman, he
believes all I say; would you would do so. Jealous of
me! I would not wrong him nor you for the world.   275

ALITHEA *walks carelessly to and fro*

SPARKISH

Look you there; hear him, hear him, and do not walk
away so.

HARCOURT

I love you, madam, so –

SPARKISH

How's that! Nay – now you begin to go too far indeed.

HARCOURT

So much, I confess, I say I love you, that I would not 280
have you miserable, and cast yourself away upon so
unworthy and inconsiderable a thing as what you see
here.   *Clapping his hand on his breast, points at* SPARKISH

SPARKISH

No, faith, I believe thou would'st not. Now his meaning
is plain. But I knew before thou would'st not wrong me 285
nor her.

HARCOURT

No, no heavens forbid the glory of her sex should fall so
low as into the embraces of such a contemptible wretch,
the least of mankind – my dear friend here – I injure him.

Embracing SPARKISH 290

---

262   *she'll make no use of her fortune* i.e., she will not cuckold him
263   *none to* there is nobody like   275   sd *carelessly* unconcernedly
289   *least* Q2–5, O (last Q1); 'last' is defensible, but 'least' is clearer.

ALITHEA

    Very well.

SPARKISH

    No, no, dear friend, I knew it. Madam, you see he will
rather wrong himself than me, in giving himself such
names.

ALITHEA

    Do not you understand him yet?   295

SPARKISH

    Yes, how modestly he speaks of himself, poor fellow.

ALITHEA

    Methinks he speaks impudently of yourself, since –
before yourself too;   insomuch that I can no longer
suffer his scurrilous abusiveness to you, no more than
his love to me.   *Offers to go* 300

SPARKISH

    Nay, nay, madam, pray stay. His love to you! Lord,
madam, has he not spoke yet plain enough?

ALITHEA

    Yes indeed, I should think so.

SPARKISH

    Well then, by the world, a man can't speak civilly to a
woman now but presently she says he makes love to her! 305
Nay, madam, you shall stay, with your pardon, since
you have not yet understood him, till he has made an
éclaircissement of his love to you, that is, what kind of
love it is.   [*To* HARCOURT]   Answer to thy catechism:
friend, do you love my mistress here?   310

HARCOURT

    Yes, I wish she would not doubt it.

SPARKISH

    But how do you love her?

HARCOURT

    With all my soul.

ALITHEA

    I thank him;   methinks he speaks plain enough now.

SPARKISH (*To* ALITHEA)

    You are out still.   – But with what kind of love, 315
Harcourt?

---

292 *it. Madam*, Q2 (it Madam, Q1; it, Madam, Q3; it: Madam, Q4–5, O)
308 *éclaircissement* elucidation; an affectation
315 *out* mistaken

HARCOURT
With the best and truest love in the world.
SPARKISH
Look you there then, that is with no matrimonial love,
I'm sure.
ALITHEA
How's that? Do you say matrimonial love is not best?   320
SPARKISH [*Aside*]
Gad, I went too far ere I was aware. – But speak for
thyself, Harcourt; you said you would not wrong me
nor her.
HARCOURT
No, no, madam, e'en take him for heaven's sake –
SPARKISH
Look you there, madam   325
HARCOURT
Who should in all justice be yours, he that loves you
most.   *Claps his hand on his breast*
ALITHEA
Look you there, Master Sparkish, who's that?
SPARKISH
Who should it be? – Go on, Harcourt.
HARCOURT
Who loves you more than women titles, or fortune fools. 330
                                            Points at SPARKISH
SPARKISH
Look you there, he means me still, for he points at me.
ALITHEA
Ridiculous!
HARCOURT
Who can only match your faith and constancy in love.
SPARKISH
Ay.
HARCOURT
Who knows, if it be possible, how to value so much 335
beauty and virtue.
SPARKISH
Ay.

---

318 *no matrimonial love* Sparkish falls into the usual cynicism about marriage.
321 sd [*Aside*] But perhaps he is foolish enough to speak openly?
330 *more than women titles, or fortune fools* more than women love titles, or
     fortune loves fools. 'Fortune favours fools' was proverbial, and is echoed
     again by Harcourt at ll. 536–7.

HARCOURT

Whose love can no more be equalled in the world than
that heavenly form of yours.

SPARKISH

No.   340

HARCOURT

Who could no more suffer a rival than your absence,
and yet could no more suspect your virtue than his own
constancy in his love to you.

SPARKISH

No.

HARCOURT

Who, in fine, loves you better than his eyes, that first 345
made him love you.

SPARKISH

Ay – nay, madam, faith, you shan't go, till –

ALITHEA

Have a care, lest you make me stay too long –

SPARKISH

But till he has saluted you; that I may be assured you
are friends, after his honest advice and declaration. 350
Come, pray, madam, be friends with him.

Enter PINCHWIFE, MRS PINCHWIFE

ALITHEA

You must pardon me, sir, that I am not yet so obedient
to you.

PINCHWIFE

What, invite your wife to kiss men? Monstrous! Are
you not ashamed? I will never forgive you.   355

SPARKISH

Are you not ashamed that I should have more
confidence in the chastity of your family than you have?
You must not teach me; I am a man of honour, sir,
though I am frank and free. I am frank, sir –

---

345 *in fine* finally, in short; French *enfin*. In Dryden's *Sir Martin Mar-
      all* (1667) Moody, who hates fashionable gallicisms, demands an
      explanation of the phrase, and is told "'Tis a phrase *à-la-mode*, Sir, and
      is used in conversation now, as a whiff of tobacco was formerly, in the
      midst of a discourse, for a thinking while' (III.i.).
349 *saluted* kissed
350 *advice* opinion
359 *frank and free* unconventional; a very vague phrase

PINCHWIFE
Very frank, sir, to share your wife with your friends.   360
SPARKISH
He is an humble, menial friend, such as reconciles the
differences of the marriage bed. You know man and
wife do not always agree; I design him for that use,
therefore would have him well with my wife.
PINCHWIFE
A menial friend! You will get a great many menial 365
friends, by showing your wife as you do.
SPARKISH
What then? It may be I have a pleasure in't, as I have to
show fine clothes at a playhouse the first day, and count
money before poor rogues.
PINCHWIFE
He that shows his wife or money will be in danger of 370
having them borrowed sometimes.
SPARKISH
I love to be envied, and would not marry a wife that I
alone could love. Loving alone is as dull as eating alone.
Is it not a frank age? And I am a frank person. And to
tell you the truth, it may be I love to have rivals in a 375
wife; they make her seem to a man still but as a kept
mistress. And so good night, for I must to Whitehall.
Madam, I hope you are now reconciled to my friend;
and so I wish you a good night, madam, and sleep if you
can, for tomorrow you know I must visit you early with a 380
canonical gentleman. Good night, dear Harcourt.

                                                  Exit SPARKISH

HARCOURT
Madam, I hope you will not refuse my visit tomorrow, if
it should be earlier, with a canonical gentleman, than
Master Sparkish's?
PINCHWIFE (*Coming between* ALITHEA *and* HARCOURT)
This gentlewoman is yet under my care; therefore you 385
must yet forbear your freedom with her, sir.
HARCOURT
Must, sir!

---

360 *frank* generous; sarcastic
361 *menial* domestic
368 *first day première* of a play
374 *frank* candid
381 *canonical gentleman* parson, to conduct the marriage ceremony

PINCHWIFE
Yes, sir, she is my sister.
HARCOURT
'Tis well she is, sir – for I must be her servant, sir.
Madam –   390
PINCHWIFE
Come away, sister. We had been gone if it had not been
for you, and so avoided these lewd rakehells who seem
to haunt us.

Enter HORNER, DORILANT *to them*

HORNER
How now, Pinchwife?
PINCHWIFE
Your servant.   395
HORNER
What! I see a little time in the country makes a man
turn wild and unsociable, and only fit to converse with
his horses, dogs, and his herds.
PINCHWIFE
I have business, sir, and must mind it. Your business is
pleasure, therefore you and I must go different ways.   400
HORNER
Well, you may go on, but this pretty young gentleman –
Takes hold of MRS PINCHWIFE
HARCOURT
The lady –
DORILANT
And the maid –
HORNER
Shall stay with us, for I suppose their business is the
same with ours, pleasure.   405
PINCHWIFE (*Aside*)
'Sdeath, he knows her, she carries it so sillily! Yet if he
does not, I should be more silly to discover it first.
ALITHEA
Pray, let us go, sir.

392 *rakehells* rakes
395 *Your servant* not a means of acknowledging the greeting, but a form for
      ending the conversation
399 *mind* attend to
406 *carries it* plays her part
407 *discover* reveal

PINCHWIFE
    Come, come.
HORNER (*To* MRS PINCHWIFE)
    Had you not rather stay with us? – Prithee, Pinchwife, 410
    who is this pretty young gentleman?
PINCHWIFE
    One to whom I'm a guardian. (*Aside*) I wish I could
    keep her out of your hands.
HORNER
    Who is he? I never saw anything so pretty in all my life.
PINCHWIFE
    Pshaw! do not look upon him so much; he's a poor 415
    bashful youth, you'll put him out of countenance.
    Come away, brother.   *Offers to take her away*
HORNER
    Oh, your brother?
PINCHWIFE
    Yes, my wife's brother. Come, come, she'll stay supper
    for us.   420
HORNER
    I thought so, for he is very like her I saw you at the play
    with, whom I told you I was in love with.
MRS PINCHWIFE (*Aside*)
    O Jeminy! Is this he that was in love with me? I am
    glad on't, I vow, for he's a curious fine gentleman, and I
    love him already too. (*To* PINCHWIFE) Is this he, bud?   425
PINCHWIFE
    Come away, come away!
HORNER
    Why, what haste are you in? Why won't you let me talk
    with him?
PINCHWIFE
    Because you'll debauch him. He's yet young and
    innocent, and I would not have him debauched for 430
    anything in the world. (*Aside*) How she gazes on him!
    The devil!
HORNER
    Harcourt, Dorilant, look you here; this is the likeness of
    that dowdy he told us of, his wife. Did you ever see a

---

419 *stay* delay
423 *O Jeminy!* corruption of Gemini;   expression often used by un-
       sophisticated characters
424 *curious* remarkably
434 *dowdy* unattractive woman

lovelier creature? The rogue has reason to be jealous of 435
his wife, since she is like him, for she would make all
that see her in love with her.

HARCOURT

And as I remember now, she is as like him here as can
be.

DORILANT

She is indeed very pretty, if she be like him.   440

HORNER

Very pretty? A very pretty commendation! She is a
glorious creature, beautiful beyond all things I ever
beheld.

PINCHWIFE

So, so.

HARCOURT

More beautiful than a poet's first mistress of imagina- 445
tion.

HORNER

Or another man's last mistress of flesh and blood.

MRS PINCHWIFE

Nay, now you jeer sir; pray don't jeer me –

PINCHWIFE

Come, come. (*Aside*) By heavens, she'll discover herself.   450

HORNER

I speak of your sister, sir.

PINCHWIFE

Ay, but saying she was handsome, if like him, made him
blush. (*Aside*) I am upon a rack!

HORNER

Methinks he is so handsome, he should not be a man.

PINCHWIFE [*Aside*]

Oh, there 'tis out, he has discovered her. I am not able 455
to suffer any longer. (*To his wife*) Come, come away, I
say.

HORNER

Nay, by your leave, sir, he shall not go yet. (*To them*)
Harcourt, Dorilant, let us torment this jealous rogue a
little.   460

HARCOURT *and* DORILANT

How?

HORNER

I'll show you.

448 *jeer* make fun (of)

PINCHWIFE

Come, pray let him go, I cannot stay fooling any longer;
I tell you his sister stays supper for us.

HORNER

Does she? Come then, we'll all go sup with her and 465
thee.

PINCHWIFE

No, now I think on't, having stayed so long for us, I
warrant she's gone to bed. (*Aside*) I wish she and I were
well out of their hands. – Come, I must rise early
tomorrow, come.   470

HORNER

Well then, if she be gone to bed, I wish her and you a
good night. But pray, young gentleman, present my
humble service to her.

MRS PINCHWIFE

Thank you heartily, sir.

PINCHWIFE (*Aside*)

'Sdeath! she will discover herself yet in spite of me. – 475
He is something more civil to you, for your kindness to
his sister, than I am, it seems.

HORNER

Tell her, dear sweet little gentleman, for all your brother
there, that you have revived the love I had for her at first
sight in the playhouse.   480

MRS PINCHWIFE

But did you love her indeed, and indeed?

PINCHWIFE (*Aside*)

So, so. – Away, I say.

HORNER

Nay, stay. Yes, indeed, and indeed, pray do you tell her
so, and give her this kiss from me.   *Kisses her*

PINCHWIFE (*Aside*)

O heavens! What do I suffer! Now 'tis too plain he 485
knows her, and yet –

HORNER

And this, and this –   *Kisses her again*

MRS PINCHWIFE

What do you kiss me for? I am no woman.

PINCHWIFE (*Aside*)

So, there 'tis out. – Come, I cannot, nor will stay any
longer.   490

HORNER

Nay, they shall send your lady a kiss too. Here
Harcourt, Dorilant, will you not?   *They kiss her*

PINCHWIFE (*Aside*)

How! do I suffer this? Was I not accusing another just
now for this rascally patience, in permitting his wife to
be kissed before his face? Ten thousand ulcers gnaw 495
away their lips! Come, come.

HORNER

Good night, dear little gentleman; madam, goodnight;
farewell, Pinchwife. (*Apart to* HARCOURT *and* DORILANT)
Did not I tell you I would raise his jealous gall?

Exeunt HORNER, HARCOURT *and* DORILANT

PINCHWIFE

So, they are gone at last! Stay, let me see first if the 500
coach be at this door.   *Exit*

HORNER, HARCOURT *and* DORILANT *return*

HORNER

What, not gone yet? Will you be sure to do as I desired
you, sweet sir?

MRS PINCHWIFE

Sweet sir, but what will you give me then?

HORNER

Anything. Come away into the next walk.   505

Exit HORNER, *haling away* MRS PINCHWIFE

ALITHEA

Hold, hold! What d'ye do?

LUCY

Stay, stay, hold –

HARCOURT

Hold, madam, hold! Let him present him, he'll come
presently; nay, I will never let you go till you answer my
question.   510

ALITHEA, LUCY, *struggling with* HARCOURT *and* DORILANT

LUCY

For god's sake, sir, I must follow 'em.

DORILANT

No, I have something to present you with too; you
shan't follow them.

PINCHWIFE *returns*

PINCHWIFE

Where? – how? – what's become of? – gone! – whither?

505 *walk* gallery of the New Exchange   sd *haling* dragging
508 *present him* give him a present
509 *presently* immediately   510 *question* that posed at ll. 382–4

LUCY

He's only gone with the gentleman, who will give him 515
something, an't please your worship.

PINCHWIFE

Something! Give him something, with a pox! – Where
are they?

ALITHEA

In the next walk only, brother.

PINCHWIFE

Only, only! Where, where?   520

Exit PINCHWIFE *and returns presently, then goes out again*

HARCOURT

What's the matter with him? Why so much concerned?
But dearest madam –

ALITHEA

Pray, let me go, sir; I have said and suffered enough
already.

HARCOURT

Then you will not look upon, nor pity, my sufferings?   525

ALITHEA

To look upon 'em, when I cannot help 'em, were
cruelty not pity; therefore I will never see you more.

HARCOURT

Let me then, madam, have my privilege of a banished
lover, complaining or railing, and giving you but a
farewell reason why, if you cannot condescend to marry 530
me, you should not take that wretch my rival.

ALITHEA

He only, not you, since my honour is engaged so far to
him, can give me a reason, why I should not marry him.
But if he be true, and what I think him to me, I must be
so to him. Your servant, sir.   535

HARCOURT

Have women only constancy when 'tis a vice, and, like
fortune, only true to fools?

DORILANT (*To* LUCY, *who struggles to get from him*)

Thou shalt not stir, thou robust creature! You see I can
deal with you, therefore you should stay the rather, and
be kind.   540

516 *an't* if it
536 *like* Q1–3 (are like Q4–5, O)
537 *fortune, only true to fools* See l. 330 above.
540 *kind* ready for sex; as at V.iv.110

Enter PINCHWIFE

PINCHWIFE

Gone, gone, not to be found! quite gone! Ten thousand
plagues go with 'em! Which way went they?

ALITHEA

But into t'other walk, brother.

LUCY

Their business will be done presently sure, an't please
your worship; it can't be long in doing, I'm sure on't.   545

ALITHEA

Are they not there?

PINCHWIFE

No; you know where they are, you infamous wretch,
eternal shame of your family, which you do not
dishonour enough yourself, you think, but you must
help her to do it too, thou legion of bawds!   550

ALITHEA

Good brother –

PINCHWIFE

Damned, damned sister!

ALITHEA

Look you here, she's coming.

Enter MRS PINCHWIFE *in man's clothes, running,*
with her hat under her arm,
full of oranges and dried fruit; HORNER *following*

MRS PINCHWIFE

O dear bud, look you here what I have got, see.

PINCHWIFE (*Aside, rubbing his forehead*)

And what I have got here too, which you can't see.   555

MRS PINCHWIFE

The fine gentleman has given me better things yet.

PINCHWIFE

Has he so? (*Aside*) Out of breath and coloured! I must
hold yet.

HORNER

I have only given your little brother an orange, sir.

PINCHWIFE (*To* HORNER)

Thank you sir.   (*Aside*) You have only squeezed my   560

___

544 *business* For the innuendo, of which Lucy may be innocent, see II.i.602.
558 *hold* restrain myself
560–1 *squeezed my orange* debauched my wife. The sexual sense is clear in,

orange, I suppose, and given it me again. Yet I must
have a city-patience. (*To his wife*) Come, come away.

MRS PINCHWIFE

Stay, till I have put up my fine things, bud.

Enter SIR JASPAR FIDGET

SIR JASPAR

O Master Horner, come, come, the ladies stay for you;
your mistress, my wife, wonders you make not more 565
haste to her.

HORNER

I have stayed this half hour for you here, and 'tis your
fault I am not now with your wife.

SIR JASPAR

But pray, don't let her know so much. The truth on't
is, I was advancing a certain project to his majesty about 570
– I'll tell you.

HORNER

No, let's go and hear it at your house. Good night,
sweet little gentleman.   One kiss more;   you'll
remember me now, I hope.   *Kisses her*

DORILANT

What, Sir Jaspar, will you separate friends?   He 575
promised to sup with us, and if you take him to your
house, you'll be in danger of our company too.

SIR JASPAR

Alas, gentlemen, my house is not fit for you; there are
none but civil women there, which are not for your
turn. He, you know, can bear with the society of civil 580
women now, ha, ha, ha! Besides, he's one of my family
– he's – he, he, he!

---

for example, John Crowne's *The Country Wit* (1676), when Ramble says
of his cuckold, 'when I had squeezed his orange, I gave him the rind
again' (II.iii). Orange wenches in the theatres were often prostitutes.

562 *city-patience* the patience of a city husband who will not admit he has
     been cuckolded. See I.i.9 and note.

562–3 Pinchwife remains on stage, but does not hear the references to
     Horner's supposed impotence (ll. 580–90).

570 *project* an absurd scheme, like those Sir Politick Would-be outlines in
     Volpone IV.i.46–125

580 *civil* respectable. For the innuendo, which does not occur to Sir Jaspar,
     see I.i.133–5.

DORILANT

What is he?

SIR JASPAR

Faith, my eunuch, since you'll have it, he, he, he!

               [*Exeunt*] SIR JASPAR FIDGET *and* HORNER

DORILANT

I rather wish thou wert his, or my cuckold. Harcourt, 585
what a good cuckold is lost there for want of a man to
make him one!   Thee and I cannot have Horner's
privilege, who can make use of it.

HARCOURT

Ay, to poor Horner 'tis like coming to an estate at three-
score, when a man can't be the better for't.   590

PINCHWIFE

Come.

MRS PINCHWIFE

Presently, bud.

DORILANT

Come, let us go too. (*To* ALITHEA)   Madam, your
servant. (*To* LUCY) Good night, strapper.

HARCOURT

Madam, though you will not let me have a good day, or 595
night, I wish you one; but dare not name the other half
of my wish.

ALITHEA

Good night, sir, for ever.

MRS PINCHWIFE

I don't know where to put this. Here, dear bud, you
shall eat it.   Nay, you shall have part of the fine 600
gentleman's good things, or treat as you call it, when we
come home.

PINCHWIFE

Indeed, I deserve it, since I furnished the best part of it.

               (*Strikes away the orange*)

The gallant treats, presents, and gives the ball;

But 'tis the absent cuckold, pays for all.   605

               · [*Exeunt*]

585   *rather wish* wish rather
594   *strapper* strapping (tall and robust) girl

Act IV, Scene i

In PINCHWIFE'*s house in the morning*
LUCY, ALITHEA *dressed in new clothes*

LUCY
  Well, madam, now have I dressed you, and set you out
  with so many ornaments, and spent upon you ounces of
  essence and pulvilio; and all this for no other purpose
  but as people adorn and perfume a corpse for a stinking
  second-hand grave, such or as bad I think Master   5
  Sparkish's bed.

ALITHEA
  Hold your peace.

LUCY
  Nay, madam, I will ask you the reason why you would
  banish poor Master Harcourt for ever from your sight?
  How could you be so hard-hearted?   10

ALITHEA
  'Twas because I was not hard-hearted.

LUCY
  No, no; 'twas stark love and kindness, I warrant.

ALITHEA
  It was so. I would see him no more, because I love him.

LUCY
  Hey-day, a very pretty reason!

ALITHEA
  You do not understand me.   15

LUCY
  I wish you may yourself.

ALITHEA
  I was engaged to marry, you see, another man, whom
  my justice will not suffer me to deceive or injure.

LUCY
  Can there be a greater cheat or wrong done to a man
  than to give him your person without your heart? I   20
  should make a conscience of it.

ALITHEA
  I'll retrieve it for him after I am married a while.

LUCY
  The woman that marries to love better will be as much

---

  3 *essence* perfume
     pulvilio perfumed powder
  21 *make a conscience of it* make it a matter of conscience not to

mistaken as the wencher that marries to live better. No,
madam, marrying to increase love is like gaming to   25
become rich; alas, you only lose what little stock you
had before.

ALITHEA

I find by your rhetoric you have been bribed to betray
me.

LUCY

Only by his merit, that has bribed your heart, you see,   30
against your word and rigid honour. But what a devil is
this honour? 'Tis sure a disease in the head, like the
megrim, or falling sickness, that always hurries people
away to do themselves mischief. Men lose their lives by
it; women what's dearer to 'em, their love, the life of   35
life.

ALITHEA

Come, pray talk you no more of honour, nor Master
Harcourt. I wish the other would come, to secure my
fidelity to him and his right in me.

LUCY

You will marry him then?   40

ALITHEA

Certainly. I have given him already my word, and will
my hand too, to make it good, when he comes.

LUCY

Well, I wish I may never stick pin more if he be not an
arrant natural to t'other fine gentleman.

ALITHEA

I own he wants the wit of Harcourt, which I will dis-   45
pense withal for another want he has, which is want of
jealousy; which men of wit seldom want.

LUCY

Lord, madam, what should you do with a fool to your
husband? You intend to be honest, don't you? Then
that husbandly virtue, credulity, is thrown away upon   50
you.

ALITHEA

He only that could suspect my virtue should have cause

33   *megrim* migraine
       falling sickness epilepsy
44   *arrant* complete
       natural born fool
45–6 *dispense withal* do without
49   *honest* chaste

to do it.   'Tis Sparkish's confidence in my truth that
obliges me to be so faithful to him.

LUCY

You are not sure his opinion may last.   55

ALITHEA

I am satisfied 'tis impossible for him to be jealous, after
the proofs I have had of him.   Jealousy in a husband,
heaven defend me from it!   It begets a thousand plagues
to a poor woman, the loss of her honour, her quiet, and
her –   60

LUCY

And her pleasure.

ALITHEA

What d'ye mean, impertinent?

LUCY

Liberty is a great pleasure, madam.

ALITHEA

I say, loss of her honour, her quiet, nay, her life
sometimes;   and what's as bad almost, the loss of this   65
town, that is, she is sent into the country, which is the
last ill usage of a husband to a wife, I think.

LUCY (*Aside*)

Oh, does the wind lie there?   – Then of necessity,
madam, you think a man must carry his wife into the
country, if he be wise.   The country is as terrible, I find,   70
to our young English ladies as a monastery to those
abroad.   And on my virginity, I think they would rather
marry a London jailer than a high sheriff of a county,
since neither can stir from his employment.   Formerly
women of wit married fools for a great estate, a fine seat,   75
or the like;   but now 'tis for a pretty seat only in
Lincoln's Inn Fields, St James's Fields, or the Pall Mall.

Enter to them SPARKISH, *and* HARCOURT
dressed like a parson

65–7 Similarly Harriet, the heroine of *The Man of Mode*, is so in love with
'this dear town' that she 'can scarce endure the country in landscapes
and in hangings' (III.i.92–3).   Such views would sound less extreme to
the original London audience.

70–2 In *L'École des Femmes* (see Introduction, p. xxvi) Agnes has been not
only brought up in the country but also educated at a convent.

77 *Lincoln's Inn Fields, St James's Fields, or the Pall Mall* fashionable places
to live.   The earls of Bristol and Sandwich lived in Lincoln's Inn Fields,
the earls of Clarendon and Oxford in St James's Square, which had been
laid out in St James's Fields, and Sir William Temple, Robert Boyle and
Nell Gwyn in Pall Mall.

SPARKISH

Madam, your humble servant, a happy day to you, and
to us all.

HARCOURT

Amen.   80

ALITHEA

Who have we here?

SPARKISH

My chaplain, faith. O madam, poor Harcourt remem-
bers his humble service to you, and in obedience to your
last commands, refrains coming into your sight.

ALITHEA

Is not that he?   85

SPARKISH

No, fie no; but to show that he ne'er intended to hinder
our match, has sent his brother here to join our hands.
When I get me a wife, I must get her a chaplain,
according to the custom. This is his brother, and my
chaplain.   90

ALITHEA

His brother?

LUCY (*Aside*)

And your chaplain, to preach in your pulpit, then!

ALITHEA

His brother!

SPARKISH

Nay, I knew you would not believe it. – I told you, sir,
she would take you for your brother Frank.   95

ALITHEA

Believe it!

LUCY (*Aside*)

His brother! ha, ha, he! He has a trick left still, it seems.

SPARKISH

Come, my dearest, pray let us go to church before the
canonical hour is past.

88–9 It seems Sparkish has engaged Harcourt permanently, as a domestic
chaplain. Macaulay describes the low status of such chaplains in *The
History of England*, ch. 3. Jeremy Collier complains of Wycherley's
abuse of the clergy here in *A Short View*, p.100; see Introduction,
pp. xxxi and xxxii.

92 *preach in your pulpit* have sex with you (Farmer and Henley, under
'pulpit'). The aside is to Alithea.

98–9 *before the canonical hour is past* before noon. The Anglican Book of
Canons allowed marriages to be solemnised in church between 8 a.m.
and noon. See also ll. 183–5 and note.

ALITHEA

For shame, you are abused still.   100

SPARKISH

By the world, 'tis strange now you are so incredulous.

ALITHEA

'Tis strange you are so credulous.

SPARKISH

Dearest of my life, hear me. I tell you this is Ned
Harcourt of Cambridge, by the world; you see he has a
sneaking college look. 'Tis true he's something like his 105
brother Frank, and they differ from each other no more
than in their age, for they were twins.

LUCY

Ha, ha, he!

ALITHEA

Your servant, sir; I cannot be so deceived, though you
are. But come, let's hear, how do you know what you 110
affirm so confidently?

SPARKISH

Why, I'll tell you all. Frank Harcourt coming to me this
morning to wish me joy and present his service to you, I
asked him if he could help me to a parson. Whereupon
he told me he had a brother in town who was in orders, 115
and he went straight away and sent him you see there,
to me.

ALITHEA

Yes, Frank goes and puts on a black coat, then tells you
he is Ned. That's all you have for't!

SPARKISH

Pshaw, pshaw! I tell you by the same token, the midwife 120
put her garter about Frank's neck to know 'em asunder,
they were so like.

ALITHEA

Frank tells you this too?

SPARKISH

Ay, and Ned there too. Nay, they are both in a story.

ALITHEA

So, so; very foolish.   125

104 *Cambridge* The clergy were educated at Oxford and Cambridge.
105 *sneaking college look*   *OED* sneaking *a.* 2 quotes J. Beaumont, *Psyche*
     (1648): 'No conventicle's sneaking cloisters hid those doctrines'.   In
     Thomas Shadwell's *The Humourists* (1670) Sneak, a domestic chaplain,
     is also 'a fellow of a college' (*dramatis personae*).
124 *in a story* tell the same story

SPARKISH

Lord, if you won't believe one, you had best try him by
your chambermaid there; for chambermaids must needs
know chaplains from other men, they are so used to
'em.

LUCY

Let's see; nay, I'll be sworn he has the canonical smirk, 130
and the filthy, clammy palm of a chaplain.

ALITHEA

Well, most reverend doctor, pray let us make an end of
this fooling.

HARCOURT

With all my soul, divine, heavenly creature, when you
please.   135

ALITHEA

He speaks like a chaplain indeed.

SPARKISH

Why, was there not 'soul', 'divine', 'heavenly' in what he
said?

ALITHEA

Once more, most impertinent black coat, cease your
persecution, and let us have a conclusion of this 140
ridiculous love.

HARCOURT (*Aside*)

I had forgot – I must suit my style to my coat, or I wear
it in vain.

ALITHEA

I have no more patience left. Let us make once an end
of this troublesome love, I say.   145

HARCOURT

So be it, seraphic lady, when your honour shall think it
meet and convenient so to do.

SPARKISH

Gad, I'm sure none but a chaplain could speak so, I
think.

127–9 Macaulay says 'the relation between divines and handmaidens was a
theme for endless jest' (*History of England,* ch. 3); Hunt quotes John
Phillips, 'There sits a chamber maid upon a hassock / Whom th'
chaplain oft instructs without his cassock' (*Satyr against Hypocrites,*
1655). But Lucy's comments, especially at ll. 162–3, suggest there was
some truth in such allegations.

144   *once* once for all

147   *so to do* Harcourt suits his style to his coat and echoes the communion
service in the *Book of Common Prayer*. 'It is meet and right so to do'.
Not being a genuine clergyman, he echoes the congregation's response.

ALITHEA

Let me tell you sir, this dull trick will not serve your 150
turn. Though you delay our marriage, you shall not
hinder it.

HARCOURT

Far be it from me, munificent patroness, to delay your
marriage. I desire nothing more than to marry you
presently, which I might do, if you yourself would; for 155
my noble, good-natured and thrice generous patron
here would not hinder it.

SPARKISH

No, poor man, not I, faith.

HARCOURT

And now, madam, let me tell you plainly, nobody else
shall marry you. By heavens, I'll die first, for I'm sure I 160
should die after it.

LUCY [*Aside*]

How his love has made him forget his function, as I
have seen it in real parsons!

ALITHEA

That was spoken like a chaplain too! Now you
understand him, I hope.   165

SPARKISH

Poor man, he takes it heinously to be refused. I can't
blame him, 'tis putting an indignity upon him not to be
suffered. But you'll pardon me, madam, it shan't be;
he shall marry us. Come away, pray, madam.

LUCY [*Aside*]

Ha, ha, he! More ado! 'Tis late.   170

ALITHEA

Invincible stupidity! I tell you he would marry me as
your rival, not as your chaplain.

SPARKISH (*Pulling her away*)

Come, come, madam.

LUCY

I pray, madam, do not refuse this reverend divine the
honour and satisfaction of marrying you; for I dare say 175
he has set his heart upon't, good doctor.

ALITHEA [*To* HARCOURT]

What can you hope or design by this?

---

161 *die after it* possibly, have orgasm after marriage. This was a common
     meaning of 'die' at the time, though the standard meaning is
     clearer.
166 *takes it heinously* is grievously offended

HARCOURT [*Aside*]

I could answer her, a reprieve for a day only often
revokes a hasty doom.   At worst, if she will not take
mercy on me and let me marry her, I have at least the   180
lover's second pleasure, hindering my rival's enjoyment,
though but for a time.

SPARKISH

Come, madam, 'tis e'en twelve o'clock, and my mother
charged me never to be married out of the canonical
hours.   Come, come!   Lord, here's such a deal of   185
modesty, I warrant, the first day.

LUCY

Yes, an't please your worship, married women show all
their modesty the first day, because married men show
all their love the first day.

Exeunt SPARKISH, ALITHEA, HARCOURT *and* LUCY

[Act IV, Scene ii]

The scene changes to a bedchamber,
where appear PINCHWIFE, MRS PINCHWIFE

PINCHWIFE

Come, tell me, I say.

MRS PINCHWIFE

Lord! ha'n't I told it an hundred times over?

PINCHWIFE (*Aside*)

I would try if, in the repetition of the ungrateful tale, I
could find her altering it in the least circumstance; for if
her story be false, she is so too.   – Come, how was't,   5
baggage?

MRS PINCHWIFE

Lord, what pleasure you take to hear it, sure!

PINCHWIFE

No, you take more in telling it, I find.   But speak – how
was't?

MRS PINCHWIFE

He carried me up into the house next to the Exchange.   10

---

183   *e'en* almost.   Normally in such a phrase the meaning would be
'precisely', but Sparkish does not seem to think he has missed the
canonical hours.
183–4   *my mother charged me* perhaps a characteristic foppish expression;
also used by Sir Simon Addleplot, *Love in a Wood* I.ii.203
  3   *ungrateful* disagreeable

PINCHWIFE

So, and you two were only in the room.

MRS PINCHWIFE

Yes, for he sent away a youth, that was there, for some
dried fruit and China oranges.

PINCHWIFE

Did he so? Damn him for it – and for –

MRS PINCHWIFE

But presently came up the gentlewoman of the house.   15

PINCHWIFE

Oh, 'twas well she did! But what did he do whilst the
fruit came?

MRS PINCHWIFE

He kissed me an hundred times, and told me he fancied
he kissed my fine sister, meaning me, you know, whom
he said he loved with all his soul, and bid me be sure to   20
tell her so, and to desire her to be at her window by
eleven of the clock this morning, and he would walk
under it at that time.

PINCHWIFE (*Aside*)

And he was as good as his word, very punctual, a pox
reward him for't.   25

MRS PINCHWIFE

Well, and he said if you were not within, he would come
up to her, meaning me, you know bud, still.

PINCHWIFE (*Aside*)

So – he knew her certainly. But for this confession I am
obliged to her simplicity. – But what, you stood very
still when he kissed you?   30

MRS PINCHWIFE

Yes, I warrant you; would you have had me discovered
myself?

PINCHWIFE

But you told me he did some beastliness to you, as you
called it. What was't?

MRS PINCHWIFE

Why, he put –   35

PINCHWIFE

What?

11 *you two were only* only you two were
13 *China oranges* sweet oranges; a delicacy. The phrase links the bawdy
    associations of oranges (III.ii.560–1 and note) and China (IV.iii.84
    and note).
16 *whilst* until

MRS PINCHWIFE

Why, he put the tip of his tongue between my lips, and
so muzzled me – and I said, I'd bite it.

PINCHWIFE

An eternal canker seize it, for a dog!

MRS PINCHWIFE

Nay, you need not be so angry with him neither, for to   40
say truth he has the sweetest breath I ever knew.

PINCHWIFE

The devil! You were satisfied with it then, and would do
it again?

MRS PINCHWIFE

Not unless he should force me.

PINCHWIFE

Force you, changeling! I tell you no woman can be   45
forced.

MRS PINCHWIFE

Yes, but she may sure by such a one as he, for he's a
proper, goodly strong man; 'tis hard, let me tell you, to
resist him.

PINCHWIFE [*Aside*]

So, 'tis plain she loves him, yet she has not love enough   50
to make her conceal it from me. But the sight of him
will increase her aversion for me, and love for him; and
that love instruct her how to deceive me and satisfy him,
all idiot as she is. Love! 'Twas he gave women first their
craft, their art of deluding. Out of nature's hands they   55
came plain, open, silly, and fit for slaves, as she and
heaven intended 'em, but damned Love – well – I must
strangle that little monster whilst I can deal with him. –
Go fetch pen, ink, and paper out of the next room.

MRS PINCHWIFE

Yes, bud.   *Exit* MRS PINCHWIFE   60

PINCHWIFE (*Aside*)

Why should women have more invention in love than
men? It can only be because they have more desires,
more soliciting passions, more lust, and more of the
devil.

38 *muzzled* kissed closely; 'a low word' (Johnson)
39 *for a dog* for behaving like a dog
45 *changeling* simpleton
56 *plain, open* straightforward, without guile
58 *little monster* Cupid
61 *invention* inventiveness
63 *soliciting* urgent

MRS PINCHWIFE *returns*

Come, minx, sit down and write.   65
MRS PINCHWIFE

Ay, dear bud, but I can't do't very well.
PINCHWIFE

I wish you could not at all.
MRS PINCHWIFE

But what should I write for?
PINCHWIFE

I'll have you write a letter to your lover.
MRS PINCHWIFE

O Lord, to the fine gentleman a letter!   70
PINCHWIFE

Yes, to the fine gentleman.
MRS PINCHWIFE

Lord, you do but jeer; sure you jest.
PINCHWIFE

I am not so merry, come, write as I bid you.
MRS PINCHWIFE

What, do you think I am a fool?
PINCHWIFE [*Aside*]

She's afraid I would not dictate any love to him,   75
therefore she's unwilling. – But you had best begin.
MRS PINCHWIFE

Indeed, and indeed, but I won't, so I won't!
PINCHWIFE

Why?
MRS PINCHWIFE

Because he's in town. You may send for him if you will.
PINCHWIFE

Very well, you would have him brought to you; is it   80
come to this? I say, take the pen and write, or you'll
provoke me.
MRS PINCHWIFE

Lord, what d'ye make a fool of me for? Don't I know
that letters are never writ but from the country to
London and from London into the country? Now, he's   85
in town and I am in town too; therefore I can't write to
him, you know.
PINCHWIFE (*Aside*)

So, I am glad it is no worse; she is innocent enough yet.
– Yes, you may, when your husband bids you, write

---

77 *so I won't* so there; childish expression

letters to people that are in town.   90
MRS PINCHWIFE
    Oh, may I so? Then I'm satisfied.
PINCHWIFE
    Come, begin. (*Dictates*) 'Sir' –
MRS PINCHWIFE
    Shan't I say 'Dear Sir'?   You know one says always
    something more than bare 'Sir'.
PINCHWIFE
    Write as I bid you, or I will write 'whore' with this   95
    penknife in your face.
MRS PINCHWIFE
    Nay, good bud. (*She writes*) 'Sir'.
PINCHWIFE
    'Though I suffered last night your nauseous, loathed
    kisses and embraces' – Write.
MRS PINCHWIFE
    Nay, why should I say so? You know I told you he had a 100
    sweet breath.
PINCHWIFE
    Write!
MRS PINCHWIFE
    Let me but put out 'loathed'.
PINCHWIFE
    Write, I say.
MRS PINCHWIFE
    Well, then. (*Writes*)   105
PINCHWIFE
    Let's see what you have writ. (*Takes the paper and reads*)
    'Though I suffered last night your kisses and embraces'.
    – Thou impudent creature!   Where is 'nauseous' and
    'loathed'?
MRS PINCHWIFE
    I can't abide to write such filthy words.   110
PINCHWIFE
    Once more write as I'd have you, and question it not, or
    I will spoil thy writing with this. (*Holds up the penknife*)
    I will stab out those eyes that cause my mischief.
MRS PINCHWIFE
    O Lord, I will!

94 *bare* merely. But perhaps the word provokes Pinchwife.
95–6 · Possibly echoes Othello: 'Was this fair paper, this most goodly book,
      / Made to write "whore" upon?' (*Othello* IV.ii.73–4).
103 *put out* cross out

PINCHWIFE

So – so – Let's see now! (*Reads*) 'Though I suffered 115
last night your nauseous, loathed kisses and embraces'.
– Go on – 'Yet I would not have you presume that you
shall ever repeat them'. – So –

MRS PINCHWIFE (*She writes*)

I have writ it.

PINCHWIFE

On then. – 'I then concealed myself from your 120
knowledge, to avoid your insolencies' –

MRS PINCHWIFE (*She writes*)

So –

PINCHWIFE

'The same reason, now I am out of your hands' –

MRS PINCHWIFE (*She writes*)

So –

PINCHWIFE

'Makes me own to you my unfortunate, though inno- 125
cent frolic, of being in man's clothes' –

MRS PINCHWIFE (*She writes*)

So –

PINCHWIFE

'that you may for ever more cease to pursue her, who
hates and detests you' –

MRS PINCHWIFE (*She writes on. Sighs*)

Soh –   130

PINCHWIFE

What, do you sigh? – 'detests you – as much as she loves
her husband and her honour'.

MRS PINCHWIFE

I vow, husband, he'll ne'er believe I should write such a
letter.

PINCHWIFE

What, he'd expect a kinder from you? Come now, your 135
name only.

MRS PINCHWIFE

What, shan't I say 'Your most faithful, humble servant
till death'?

PINCHWIFE

No, tormenting fiend! (*Aside*) Her style, I find, would
be very soft. – Come, wrap it up now, whilst I go fetch 140

135 *kinder* more loving
139 *style* formal conclusion
140 *soft* mollifying

wax and a candle, and write on the back side 'For
Master Horner'.

Exit PINCHWIFE

MRS PINCHWIFE

'For Master Horner' – So, I am glad he has told me his
name. Dear Master Horner! But why should I send
thee such a letter that will vex thee and make thee angry 145
with me? – Well, I will not send it. – Ay, but then my
husband will kill me – for I see plainly, he won't let me
love Master Horner – but what care I for my husband?
– I won't, so I won't send poor Master Horner such a
letter – but then my husband – But oh, what if I writ at 150
bottom, my husband made me write it? – Ay, but then
my husband would see't – Can one have no shift? Ah, a
London woman would have had a hundred presently.
Stay – what if I should write a letter, and wrap it up like
this, and write upon't too? Ay, but then my husband 155
would see't – I don't know what to do – But yet i'vads
I'll try, so I will – for I will not send this letter to poor
Master Horner, come what will on't.

(*She writes, and repeats what she hath writ*)
'Dear Sweet Master Horner' – so – 'My husband would
have me send you a base, rude, unmannerly letter – but 160
I won't' – so – 'and would have me forbid you loving me
– but I won't' – so – 'and would have me say to you, I
hate you poor Master Horner – but I won't tell a lie for
him' – there – 'for I'm sure if you and I were in the
country at cards together' – so – 'I could not help 165
treading on your toe under the table' – so – 'or rubbing
knees with you, and staring in your face till you saw me'
– very well – 'and then looking down and blushing for an
hour together' – so – 'but I must make haste before my
husband come; and now he has taught me to write 170
letters, you shall have longer ones from me, who am,
dear, dear, poor dear Master Horner, your most humble
friend, and servant to command till death, Margery
Pinchwife'. – Stay, I must give him a hint at bottom –
so – now wrap it up just like t'other – so – now write 175
'For Master Horner'. – But, oh now, what shall I do
with it? For here comes my husband.

152   *shift* expedient
156   *i'vads* in faith; rustic oath
174   *hint at bottom* i.e., the postscript read by Horner at IV.iii.286–9

Enter PINCHWIFE

PINCHWIFE (*Aside*)

I have been detained by a sparkish coxcomb, who
pretended a visit to me; but I fear 'twas to my wife. –
What, have you done?   180

MRS PINCHWIFE

Ay, ay, bud, just now.

PINCHWIFE

Let's see't. What d'ye tremble for? What, you would
not have it go?

MRS PINCHWIFE

Here. (*Aside*) No, I must not give him that. (*He opens
and reads the first letter*) So I had been served if I had   185
given him this.

PINCHWIFE

Come, where's the wax and seal?

MRS PINCHWIFE (*Aside*)

Lord, what shall I do now? Nay, then, I have it. – Pray,
let me see't. Lord, you think me so arrant a fool I
cannot seal a letter? I will do't, so I will.   190

> *Snatches the letter from him, changes it for the other,*
> *seals it, and delivers it to him*

PINCHWIFE

Nay, I believe you will learn that, and other things too,
which I would not have you.

MRS PINCHWIFE

So. Ha'n't I done it curiously? (*Aside*) I think I have;
there's my letter going to Master Horner, since he'll
needs have me send letters to folks.   195

PINCHWIFE

'Tis very well; but I warrant, you would not have it go
now?

MRS PINCHWIFE

Yes, indeed, but I would, bud, now.

PINCHWIFE

Well you are a good girl then. Come, let me lock you up
in your chamber till I come back. And be sure you   200
come not within three strides of the window when I am

---

178 *sparkish coxcomb* fop, like Sparkish himself. See note to 'The Persons',
   p. 4.
184 *that* i.e., the second letter. She almost hands him the wrong one.
185–6 That is what would have happened if I had given him the second letter,
   i.e., he would have read it.
193 *curiously* carefully

gone, for I have a spy in the street.

Exit MRS PINCHWIFE; PINCHWIFE *locks the door*

At least, 'tis fit she think so. If we do not cheat women, they'll cheat us; and fraud may be justly used with secret enemies, of which a wife is the most dangerous. 205 And he that has a handsome one to keep, and a frontier town, must provide against treachery rather than open force. Now I have secured all within I'll deal with the foe without with false intelligence.

Holds up the letter
Exit PINCHWIFE

[Act IV, Scene iii]

The scene changes to HORNER*'s lodging*
QUACK *and* HORNER

QUACK

Well, sir, how fadges the new design? Have you not the luck of all your brother projectors, to deceive only yourself at last?

HORNER

No, good domine doctor, I deceive you, it seems, and others too, for the grave matrons and old rigid husbands 5 think me as unfit for love as they are. But their wives, sisters and daughters know some of 'em better things already.

QUACK

Already!

HORNER

Already, I say. Last night I was drunk with half a dozen 10 of your civil persons, as you call 'em, and people of honour, and so was made free of their society and dressing rooms for ever hereafter; and am already come to the privileges of sleeping upon their pallets, warming smocks, tying shoes and garters, and the like, doctor, 15

206 *and* and she
209 *false intelligence* disinformation
  1 *fadges* gets on
  2 *projectors* schemers. Sir Jaspar, for example, has boasted of 'a certain project' of his (III.ii.570), presumably a crazy scheme.
  4 *domine* master; polite address to a member of a learned profession, here used ironically
 14 *pallets* straw mattresses or inferior beds

already, already, doctor.

QUACK

You have made use of your time, sir.

HORNER

I tell thee, I am now no more interruption to 'em when
they sing or talk bawdy than a little squab French page
who speaks no English.   20

QUACK

But do civil persons and women of honour drink and
sing bawdy songs?

HORNER

Oh, amongst friends, amongst friends. For your bigots
in honour are just like those in religion. They fear the
eye of the world more than the eye of heaven, and think   25
there is no virtue but railing at vice, and no sin but
giving scandal. They rail at a poor, little, kept player,
and keep themselves some young, modest pulpit
comedian to be privy to their sins in their closets, not to
tell 'em of them in their chapels.   30

QUACK

Nay, the truth on't is, priests amongst the women now
have quite got the better of us lay confessors, physicians.

HORNER

And they are rather their patients, but –

Enter my LADY FIDGET, *looking about her*

Now we talk of women of honour, here comes one. Step
behind the screen there, and but observe if I have not   35
particular privileges with the women of reputation
already, doctor, already.   [QUACK *steps behind screen*]

LADY FIDGET

Well, Horner, am not I a woman of honour? You see,
I'm as good as my word.

HORNER

And you shall see, madam, I'll not be behindhand with   40
you in honour. And I'll be as good as my word too, if
you please but to withdraw into the next room.

LADY FIDGET

But first, my dear sir, you must promise to have a care of
my dear honour.

---

19 *squab* chubby
27 *kept player* See II.i.360–5 and notes.
28–9 *pulpit comedian* domestic chaplain. See IV.i.88–92 and notes.

HORNER

If you talk a word more of your honour, you'll make me   45
incapable to wrong it.   To talk of honour in the
mysteries of love is like talking of heaven or the deity in
an operation of witchcraft, just when you are employing
the devil; it makes the charm impotent.

LADY FIDGET

Nay, fie, let us not be smutty. But you talk of mysteries   50
and bewitching to me; I don't understand you.

HORNER

I tell you, madam, the word 'money' in a mistress's
mouth, at such a nick of time, is not a more
disheartening sound to a younger brother than that of
honour to an eager lover like myself.   55

LADY FIDGET

But you can't blame a lady of my reputation to be chary.

HORNER

Chary! I have been chary of it already, by the report I
have caused of myself.

LADY FIDGET

Ay, but if you should ever let other women know that
dear secret, it would come out. Nay, you must have a   60
great care of your conduct, for my acquaintance are so
censorious – oh 'tis a wicked censorious world, Master
Horner! – I say, are so censorious and detracting that
perhaps they'll talk to the prejudice of my honour,
though you should not let them know the dear secret.   65

HORNER

Nay, madam, rather than they shall prejudice your
honour, I'll prejudice theirs; and to serve you, I'll lie
with 'em all, make the secret their own, and then they'll
keep it: I am a Machiavel in love, madam.

LADY FIDGET

Oh no, sir, not that way.   70

HORNER

Nay, the devil take me, if censorious women are to be
silenced any other way!

LADY FIDGET

A secret is better kept, I hope, by a single person than a
multitude. Therefore pray do not trust anybody else with

---

54 *younger brother* traditionally short of money, since elder brothers inherited
69 *Machiavel* Machiavellian, unscrupulous plotter

it, dear, dear Master Horner.   (*Embracing him*)   75

Enter SIR JASPAR FIDGET

SIR JASPAR

How now!

LADY FIDGET (*Aside*)

O my husband! – prevented! – and what's almost as
bad, found with my arms about another man – that will
appear too much – what shall I say? – Sir Jaspar, come
hither. I am trying if Master Horner were ticklish, and   80
he's as ticklish as can be. I love to torment the
confounded toad. Let you and I tickle him.

SIR JASPAR

No, your ladyship will tickle him better without me, I
suppose. But is this your buying china? I thought you
had been at the china house?   85

HORNER (*Aside*)

China house! That's my cue, I must take it. – A pox!
Can't you keep your impertinent wives at home? Some
men are troubled with the husbands, but I with the
wives. But I'd have you to know, since I cannot be your
journeyman by night, I will not be your drudge by day,   90
to squire your wife about and be your man of straw, or
scarecrow, only to pies and jays that would be nibbling
at your forbidden fruit. I shall be shortly the hackney
gentleman-usher of the town.

75 sd *Embracing him* Q1-3 (*omitted*, Q4-5, O). Perhaps in later pro-
    ductions the scene was played in a less sexy manner; see Introduction,
    p. xxxi.

84 *buying china* Collecting china was fashionable, but an association
    between china, Horner, and sex, first hinted at IV.ii.13, develops from
    here to l. 204 below. China was usually associated with women and
    virginity; see Aubrey Williams, 'The "Fall" of China and *The Rape of the
    Lock*', *Philological Quarterly*, vol. 41 (1962), 412–25, reprinted in *The
    Rape of the Lock, A Selection of Critical Essays*, ed. John Dixon Hunt
    (1968).

85 *china house* china shop. A likely place for an assignation – see V.iv.145–6
    – though the thought does not strike Sir Jaspar.

90 *journeyman* hireling. The term often had sexual connotations, as here.
    drudge hard worker; another term with sexual connotations. See
    Shakespeare, Sonnet 151, for an especially clear example.

92 *pies* magpies; *pies and jays* fops

93 *hackney* hired

94 *gentleman-usher* See II.i.499 note.

SIR JASPAR (*Aside*)

    He, he, he! Poor fellow, he's in the right on't, faith! To   95
squire women about for other folks is as ungrateful an
employment as to tell money for other folks. – He, he,
he! Ben't angry, Horner.

LADY FIDGET

    No, 'tis I have more reason to be angry, who am left by
you to go abroad indecently alone; or, what is more 100
indecent, to pin myself upon such ill-bred people of your
acquaintance as this is.

SIR JASPAR

    Nay, prithee, what has he done?

LADY FIDGET

    Nay, he has done nothing.

SIR JASPAR

    But what d'ye take ill, if he has done nothing?   105

LADY FIDGET

    Ha, ha, ha! Faith, I can't but laugh, however. Why,
d'ye think, the unmannerly toad would not come down
to me to the coach. I was fain to come up to fetch him,
or go without him, which I was resolved not to do; for
he knows china very well, and has himself very good, but 110
will not let me see it lest I should beg some. But I will
find it out, and have what I came for yet.

                Exit LADY FIDGET *and locks the door,*
                          followed by HORNER *to the door*

HORNER (*Apart to* LADY FIDGET)

    Lock the door, madam. – So, she has got into my
chamber and locked me out. Oh, the impertinency of
womankind! Well, Sir Jaspar, plain dealing is a jewel. If 115
ever you suffer your wife to trouble me again here, she
shall carry you home a pair of horns, by my Lord Mayor
she shall! Though I cannot furnish you myself, you are
sure, yet I'll find a way.

SIR JASPAR (*Aside*)

    Ha, ha, he! At my first coming in and finding her arms 120

---

96 *ungrateful* thankless. This echoes Pinchwife, IV.ii.3.

97 *tell* count

100 *indecently* unbecomingly

104, 105 *nothing* word with bawdy associations unknown to Sir Jaspar. For
instance in *Hamlet* 'nothing' is 'a fair thought to lie between maids' legs'
(III.ii.112–13).

115 *plain dealing is a jewel* proverbial. On the evidence of *The Plain Dealer* it
may be doubted if Wycherley himself wholly accepted the idea.

about him, <u>tickling him it seems</u>, I was half jealous, but
now I see my folly. –He, he, he! Poor Horner.

HORNER [*Aside*]

Nay, though you laugh now, 'twill be my turn ere long.
– Oh, women, more impertinent, more cunning and
more mischievous than their monkeys, and to me almost 125
as ugly! Now is she throwing my things about, and
rifling all I have, but I'll get into her the back way, and
so rifle her for it.

SIR JASPAR

Ha, ha, ha! Poor angry Horner.

HORNER

Stay here a little, I'll ferret her out to you presently, I 130
warrant.

Exit HORNER *at t'other door.*

SIR JASPAR

Wife! My Lady Fidget! Wife! He is coming into you
the back way!

SIR JASPAR *calls through the door to his wife;*
she answers from within

LADY FIDGET

Let him come, and welcome, which way he will.

SIR JASPAR

He'll catch you, and use you roughly, and be too strong 135
for you.

LADY FIDGET

Don't you trouble yourself, let him if he can.

QUACK (*Behind*)

This indeed I could not have believed from him, nor any
but my own eyes.

Enter Mrs SQUEAMISH

125 *monkeys* fashionable pets
127 *the back way* perhaps already a *double entendre* referring to anal inter-
     course, as in ll. 132–4. See note on l. 128 and Richard Levin, *Notes and
     Queries,* vol. 208 (1963), 338–40 and 428–9. Levin does not mention
     Wycherley's likely source in *Volpone* II.vi.58–61.
128 *rifle* *double entendre:* 'to coit with, or to caress sexually, a woman'
     (Partridge)
130 *ferret her out* get her out as a ferret does, by going in at one hole so
     that the creature comes out at another; probably with bawdy
     associations, as in Shakespeare's *Henry V*: ' I'll ... firk him, and ferret
     him' (IV.iv.27–8)
132–4 See l. 127, note.

SQUEAMISH

Where's this woman-hater, this toad, this ugly, greasy, 140
dirty sloven?

SIR JASPAR [*Aside*]

So the women all will have him ugly. Methinks he is a
comely person, but his wants make his form
contemptible to 'em; and 'tis e'en as my wife said
yesterday, talking of him, that a proper handsome 145
eunuch was as ridiculous a thing as a gigantic coward.

SQUEAMISH

Sir Jaspar, your servant. Where is the odious beast?

SIR JASPAR

He's within in his chamber, with my wife; she's playing
the wag with him.

SQUEAMISH

Is she so? And he's a clownish beast, he'll give her no 150
quarter, he'll play the wag with her again, let me tell
you. Come, let's go help her. – What, the door's
locked?

SIR JASPAR

Ay, my wife locked it.

SQUEAMISH

Did she so? Let us break it open then.   155

SIR JASPAR

No, no, he'll do her no hurt.

SQUEAMISH

No. (*Aside*) But is there no other way to get into 'em?
Whither goes this? I will disturb 'em.

                    Exit SQUEAMISH *at another door*

                    Enter OLD LADY SQUEAMISH

OLD LADY SQUEAMISH

Where is this harlotry, this impudent baggage, this
rambling tomrig? O Sir Jaspar, I'm glad to see you here. 160
Did you not see my vild grandchild come in hither just
now?

148–9 *playing the wag* being amusingly mischievous, and/or having sex. See
Partridge, *Shakespeare's Bawdy,* under 'wag'. As he was at I.i.73 Sir
Jaspar is innocent of any bawdy meaning, but Mrs Squeamish's
repetition of the phrase at l. 151 suggests that her understanding is not
altogether literal, contrary to what Horner says at l. 207.

159 *harlotry* harlot; vaguely abusive

160 *rambling* See II.i.399 note.
    tomrig bold or immodest woman (*OED,* tomboy, 2)

161 *vild* ed. (vil'd Q1–5, O) vile, depraved (*OED*). I have retained the

SIR JASPAR
  Yes.
OLD LADY SQUEAMISH
  Ay, but where is she then? where is she? Lord, Sir
  Jaspar, I have e'en rattled myself to pieces in pursuit of 165
  her. But can you tell what she makes here? They say
  below, no woman lodges here.
SIR JASPAR
  No.
OLD LADY SQUEAMISH
  No! What does she here then? Say, if it be not a
  woman's lodging, what makes she here? But are you 170
  sure no woman lodges here?
SIR JASPAR
  No, nor no man neither, this is Master Horner's lodging.
OLD LADY SQUEAMISH
  Is it so, are you sure?
SIR JASPAR
  Yes, yes.
OLD LADY SQUEAMISH
  So – then there's no hurt in't, I hope. But where is he?   175
SIR JASPAR
  He's in the next room with my wife.
OLD LADY SQUEAMISH
  Nay, if you trust him with your wife, I may with my
  Biddy. They say he's a merry harmless man now, e'en
  as harmless a man as ever came out of Italy with a good
  voice, and as pretty harmless company for a lady as a 180
  snake without his teeth.
SIR JASPAR
  Ay, ay, poor man.

                    Enter Mrs SQUEAMISH

SQUEAMISH
  I can't find 'em. – Oh, are you here, grandmother? I
  followed, you must know, my Lady Fidget hither. 'Tis
  the prettiest lodging, and I have been staring on the 185
  prettiest pictures.

---

      archaic form, as suited to Old Lady Squeamish.
166 *what she makes* what she is doing
178 *Biddy* young woman (Partridge); or abbreviation of Bridget
179–80 *as harmless … good voice* as harmless as a castrato. These singers were
      very fashionable.
186 *pictures* perhaps pornographic. See I.i.95 and note.

Enter LADY FIDGET *with a piece of china in her hand,*
and HORNER *following*

LADY FIDGET
And I have been toiling and moiling for the prettiest
piece of china, my dear.
HORNER
Nay, she has been too hard for me, do what I could.
SQUEAMISH
O Lord, I'll have some china too. Good Master Horner, 190
don't think to give other people china, and me none.
Come in with me too.
HORNER
Upon my honour I have none left now.
SQUEAMISH
Nay, nay, I have known you deny your china before
now, but you shan't put me off so. Come.   195
HORNER
This lady had the last there.
LADY FIDGET
Yes indeed, madam, to my certain knowledge he has no
more left.
SQUEAMISH
Oh, but it may be he may have some you could not find.
LADY FIDGET
What, d'ye think if he had had any left, I would not have 200
had it too? For we women of quality never think we
have china enough.
HORNER
Do not take it ill, I cannot make china for you all, but I
will have a roll-wagon for you too, another time.
SQUEAMISH
Thank you, dear toad.   205
LADY FIDGET (*To* HORNER, *aside*)
What do you mean by that promise?

187 *toiling and moiling* working hard
204 *roll-wagon* a cylindrical china vase, somewhat phallic in appearance.
      See R. J. Charleston, *Apollo*, vol. 65 (1957), 251.
205–7 As Horner replies to Lady Fidget in an aside, her question is pre-
      sumably an aside to him. But in Q1 the sd '*To* Horn, *aside*' is moved to
      the line above, presumably to save space, and this arrangement persists
      in Q2–5, O, even where there is no need to save space. Hence some
      editors give the aside to Mrs Squeamish, but there seems to be no reason
      why she should not speak openly.

HORNER (*Apart to* LADY FIDGET)
Alas, she has an innocent, literal understanding.
OLD LADY SQUEAMISH
Poor Master Horner, he has enough to do to please you
all, I see.
HORNER
Ay, madam, you see how they use me.   210
OLD LADY SQUEAMISH
Poor gentleman, I pity you.
HORNER
I thank you madam. I could never find pity but from
such reverend ladies as you are. The young ones will
never spare a man.
SQUEAMISH
Come, come, beast, and go dine with us, for we shall 215
want a man at ombre after dinner.
HORNER
That's all their use of me, madam, you see.
SQUEAMISH
Come, sloven, I'll lead you, to be sure of you.
                                   Pulls him by the cravat
OLD LADY SQUEAMISH
Alas, poor man, how she tugs him! Kiss, kiss her!
That's the way to make such nice women quiet.   220
HORNER
No, madam, that remedy is worse than the torment.
They know I dare suffer anything rather than do it.
OLD LADY SQUEAMISH
Prithee kiss her, and I'll give you her picture in little,
that you admired so last night. Prithee, do!
HORNER
Well, nothing but that could bribe me. I love a woman 225
only in effigy, and good painting, as much as I hate
them. I'll do't, for I could adore the devil well painted.
                                   Kisses Mrs SQUEAMISH
SQUEAMISH
Foh! you filthy toad! Nay, now I've done jesting.
OLD LADY SQUEAMISH
Ha, ha, ha! I told you so.
SQUEAMISH
Foh! a kiss of his –   230

---

216 *want a man at ombre* See II.i.473 and note.
220 *nice* fastidious about reputation
223 *picture in little* miniature

SIR JASPAR
Has no more hurt in't than one of my spaniel's.
SQUEAMISH
Nor no more good neither.
QUACK (*Behind*)
I will now believe anything he tells me.

Enter PINCHWIFE

LADY FIDGET
O Lord, here's a man! Sir Jaspar, my mask, my mask! I
would not be seen here for the world.   235
SIR JASPAR
What, not when I am with you?
LADY FIDGET
No, no, my honour – let's be gone.
SQUEAMISH
Oh, grandmother, let us be gone. Make haste, make
haste! I know not how he may censure us!
LADY FIDGET
Be found in the lodging of anything like a man! Away!   240
Exeunt SIR JASPAR, LADY FIDGET,
OLD LADY SQUEAMISH, *Mrs* SQUEAMISH

QUACK (*Behind*)
What's here, another cuckold? He looks like one, and
none else sure have any business with him.
HORNER
Well, what brings my dear friend hither?
PINCHWIFE
Your impertinency.
HORNER
My impertinency! Why, you gentlemen that have got 245
handsome wives think you have a privilege of saying
anything to your friends, and are as brutish as if you
were our creditors.
PINCHWIFE
No, sir, I'll ne'er trust you any way.
HORNER
But why not, dear Jack? Why diffide in me thou know'st 250
so well?
PINCHWIFE
Because I do know you so well.

250 *diffide in* distrust

HORNER
Ha'n't I been always thy friend, honest Jack, always ready
to serve thee, in love or battle, before thou wert married,
and am so still?   255
PINCHWIFE
I believe so. You would be my second now indeed.
HORNER
Well, then, dear Jack, why so unkind, so grum, so
strange to me? Come, prithee kiss me, dear rogue.
Gad, I was always, I say, and am still as much thy
servant as –   260
PINCHWIFE
As I am yours, sir. What, you would send a kiss to my
wife, is that it?
HORNER
So, there 'tis. A man can't show his friendship to a
married man, but presently he talks of his wife to you.
Prithee, let thy wife alone, and let thee and I be all one, 265
as we were wont. What, thou art as shy of my kindness
as a Lombard Street alderman of a courtier's civility at
Locket's.
PINCHWIFE
But you are overkind to me, as kind as if I were your
cuckold already. Yet I must confess you ought to be 270
kind and civil to me, since I am so kind, so civil to you,
as to bring you this. Look you there, sir.
                                        Delivers him a letter
HORNER
What is't?
PINCHWIFE
Only a love letter, sir.
HORNER
From whom? – How! this is from your wife! (*Reads*) 275
Hum – and hum –

254 *battle* duels; or so understood by Pinchwife, l. 256
258 *strange* distant
     kiss me On this custom among fashionable gentlemen the Orange-
     Woman in *The Man of Mode* comments: 'Lord what a filthy trick these
     men have got of kissing one another! *She spits*' (I.i.61–2).
265 *all one* friends
266 *shy* suspicious
267 *Lombard Street alderman* a banker or moneylender, who would suspect a
     courtier of avoiding a debt, or wanting a loan, or trying to cuckold him
268 *Locket's* fashionable restaurant
269–70 See I.i.495.

PINCHWIFE

Even from my wife, sir. Am I not wondrous kind and
civil to you now too? (*Aside*) But you'll not think her so!

HORNER (*Aside*)

Ha! Is this a trick of his or hers?

PINCHWIFE

The gentleman's surprised, I find. What, you expected 280
a kinder letter?

HORNER

No, faith, not I, how could I?

PINCHWIFE

Yes, yes, I'm sure you did. A man so well made as you
are must needs be disappointed, if the women declare
not their passion at first sight or opportunity.   285

HORNER (*Aside*)

But what should this mean? Stay, the postscript.
(*Reads*) 'Be sure you love me whatsoever my husband
says to the contrary, and let him not see this, lest he
should come home and pinch me, or kill my squirrel'. It
seems he knows not what the letter contains.   290

PINCHWIFE

Come, ne'er wonder at it so much.

HORNER

Faith, I can't help it.

PINCHWIFE

Now, I think I have deserved your infinite friendship
and kindness and have showed myself sufficiently an
obliging friend and husband. Am I not so, to bring a 295
letter from my wife to her gallant?

HORNER

Ay, the devil take me, art thou the most obliging, kind
friend and husband in the world, ha, ha!

PINCHWIFE

Well, you may be merry, sir, but in short I must tell you,
sir, my honour will suffer no jesting.   300

HORNER

What dost thou mean?

PINCHWIFE

Does the letter want a comment? Then know, sir,
though I have been so civil a husband as to bring you a
letter from my wife, to let you kiss and court her to my
face, I will not be a cuckold, sir, I will not.   305

299 *merry* facetious

HORNER

Thou art mad with jealousy. I never saw thy wife in my
life, but at the play yesterday, and I know not if it were
she or no. I court her, kiss her!

PINCHWIFE

I will not be a cuckold, I say. There will be danger in
making me a cuckold. 310

HORNER

Why, wert thou not well cured of thy last clap?

PINCHWIFE

I wear a sword.

HORNER

It should be taken from thee lest thou should'st do
thyself a mischief with it. Thou art mad, man.

PINCHWIFE

As mad as I am, and as merry as you are, I must have 315
more reason from you ere we part. I say again, though
you kissed and courted last night my wife in man's
clothes, as she confesses in her letter –

HORNER (*Aside*)

Ha!

PINCHWIFE

Both she and I say, you must not design it again, for you 320
have mistaken your woman, as you have done your man.

HORNER (*Aside*)

Oh! I understand something now. – Was that thy wife?
Why would'st thou not tell me 'twas she? Faith, my
freedom with her was your fault, not mine.

PINCHWIFE (*Aside*)

Faith, so 'twas. 325

HORNER

Fie! I'd never do't to a woman before her husband's
face, sure.

PINCHWIFE

But I had rather you should do't to my wife before my
face than behind my back, and that you shall never do.

HORNER

No – you will hinder me. 330

PINCHWIFE

If I would not hinder you, you see by her letter, she
would.

311 *clap* gonorrhoea   316 *reason* explanation
322 *something* i.e., that Pinchwife thinks he has brought a different letter. He
pretends he has just understood that it was Mrs Pinchwife in man's
clothes.

HORNER

Well, I must e'en acquiesce then, and be contented with
what she writes.

PINCHWIFE

I'll assure you 'twas voluntarily writ. I had no hand in't, 335
you may believe me.

HORNER

I do believe thee, faith.

PINCHWIFE

And believe her too, for she's an innocent creature, has
no dissembling in her; and so fare you well, sir.

HORNER

Pray, however, present my humble service to her, and 340
tell her I will obey her letter to a tittle, and fulfil her
desires, be what they will, or with what difficulty soever I
do't, and you shall be no more jealous of me, I warrant
her, and you –

PINCHWIFE

Well, then, fare you well, and play with any man's 345
honour but mine, kiss any man's wife but mine, and
welcome.

Exit PINCHWIFE

HORNER

Ha, ha, ha! Doctor.

QUACK

It seems he has not heard the report of you, or does not
believe it.   350

HORNER

Ha, ha! Now, doctor, what think you?

QUACK

Pray let's see the letter – hum – (*Reads the letter*) 'for –
dear – love you' –

HORNER

I wonder how she could contrive it! What say'st thou
to't? 'Tis an original.   355

QUACK

So are your cuckolds, too, originals, for they are like no
other common cuckolds, and I will henceforth believe it
not impossible for you to cuckold the Grand Signior
amidst his guards of eunuchs, that I say –

341 *to a tittle* in every particular
355 *an original* her own work, not a copy. The same word is used by
     Ergaste of Isabelle's letter in *L'École des Maris* II.v.
358 *Grand Signior* Sultan of Turkey; also mentioned at II.i.471–2

HORNER

And I say for the letter, 'tis the first love letter that ever 360
was without flames, darts, fates, destinies, lying and
dissembling in't.

Enter SPARKISH *pulling in* PINCHWIFE

SPARKISH

Come back, you are a pretty brother-in-law, neither go
to church, nor to dinner with your sister bride.

PINCHWIFE

My sister denies her marriage, and you see is gone away 365
from you dissatisfied.

SPARKISH

Pshaw! upon a foolish scruple that our parson was not
in lawful orders, and did not say all the Common
Prayer. But 'tis her modesty only, I believe. But let
women be never so modest the first day, they'll be sure 370
to come to themselves by night, and I shall have enough
of her then. In the meantime, Harry Horner, you must
dine with me. I keep my wedding at my aunt's in the
Piazza.

HORNER

Thy wedding! What stale maid has lived to despair of a 375
husband, or what young one of a gallant?

SPARKISH

Oh, your servant, sir – this gentleman's sister then – no
stale maid.

HORNER

I'm sorry for't.

PINCHWIFE (*Aside*)

How comes he so concerned for her?   380

SPARKISH

You sorry for't? Why, do you know any ill by her?

HORNER

No, I know none but by thee. 'Tis for her sake, not
yours, and another man's sake that might have hoped, I
thought –

SPARKISH

Another man! Another man! What is his name?   385

368–9 *Common Prayer* marriage service in the Anglican *Book of Common
     Prayer*
374 *Piazza* arcade near Covent Garden. V.iii. is located there.
375 *stale* past her best

HORNER

Nay, since 'tis past he shall be nameless. (*Aside*) Poor
Harcourt! I am sorry thou hast missed her.

PINCHWIFE (*Aside*)

He seems to be much troubled at the match.

SPARKISH

Prithee tell me – nay, you shan't go, brother.

PINCHWIFE

I must of necessity, but I'll come to you to dinner.   390

Exit PINCHWIFE

SPARKISH

But Harry, what, have I rival in my wife already? But
with all my heart, for he may be of use to me hereafter.
For though my hunger is now my sauce, and I can fall
on heartily without, but the time will come when a rival
will be as good sauce for a married man to a wife as an   395
orange to veal.

HORNER

O thou damned rogue, thou hast set my teeth on edge
with thy orange!

SPARKISH

Then let's to dinner – there I was with you again.
Come.   400

HORNER

But who dines with thee?

SPARKISH

My friends and relations, my brother Pinchwife, you
see, of your acquaintance.

HORNER

And his wife?

SPARKISH

No, gad, he'll ne'er let her come amongst us good   405
fellows. Your stingy country coxcomb keeps his wife
from his friends as he does his little firkin of ale for his
own drinking, and a gentleman can't get a smack on't.
But his servants, when his back is turned, broach it at
their pleasures, and dust it away, ha, ha, ha! Gad, I am   410
witty, I think, considering I was married today, by the
world. But come –

387   *missed* lost
399   *was with you* had you
407   *firkin* cask
408   *smack* taste
410   *dust it away* toss it off; with a sexual innuendo

HORNER

No, I will not dine with you, unless you can fetch her
too.

SPARKISH

Pshaw! what pleasure canst thou have with women now 415
Harry?

HORNER

My eyes are not gone; I love a good prospect yet, and
will not dine with you unless she does too. Go fetch her,
therefore, but do not tell her husband 'tis for my sake.

SPARKISH

Well, I'll go try what I can do. In the meantime come 420
away to my aunt's lodging, 'tis in the way to Pinchwife's.

HORNER [*Aside to* QUACK]

The poor woman has called for aid, and stretched forth
her hand, doctor. I cannot but help her over the pale
out of the briars.

Exeunt SPARKISH, HORNER, QUACK

[Act IV, Scene iv]

The scene changes to PINCHWIFE'*s house*
MRS PINCHWIFE *alone leaning on her elbow. A table,*
pen, ink, and paper

MRS PINCHWIFE

Well, 'tis e'en so, I have got the London disease they call
love. I am sick of my husband, and for my gallant. I
have heard this distemper called a fever, but methinks
'tis liker an ague, for when I think of my husband I
tremble and am in a cold sweat, and have inclinations to   5
vomit, but when I think of my gallant, dear Master
Horner, my hot fit comes and I am all in a fever, indeed,
and as in other fevers my own chamber is tedious to me,
and I would fain be removed to his, and then methinks I
should be well. Ah, poor Master Horner! Well, I   10

423 *pale*   (literally)   fence,   (metaphorically)   boundary,   especially
      boundary of civilisation
424 *briars*   (literally)   prickly   bushes,   (metaphorically)   difficulties,   'with
      conscious reference to the literal sense' (*OED* brier *sb.*¹ 4)
   2 *for* i.e., sick for
   3 *distemper* unbalanced state, disease
   4 *ague* type of fever recognised by successive cold shivering and hot
      feverish symptoms

cannot, will not stay here. Therefore I'll make an end of
my letter to him, which shall be a finer letter than my
last, because I have studied it like anything. Oh, sick,
sick!   *Takes the pen and writes*

Enter PINCHWIFE, *who seeing her writing*
steals softly behind her, and looking over her shoulder,
snatches the paper from her

PINCHWIFE
What, writing more letters?   15
MRS PINCHWIFE
O Lord, bud, why d'ye fright me so?
                    She offers to run out; he stops her and reads
PINCHWIFE
How's this! Nay, you shall not stir, madam. 'Dear, dear,
dear Master Horner' – very well! – I have taught you to
write letters to good purpose – but let's see't – 'First, I
am to beg your pardon for my boldness in writing to   20
you, which I'd have you to know I would not have done,
had not you said first you loved me so extremely, which
if you do, you will never suffer me to lie in the arms of
another man, whom I loathe, nauseate, and detest' –
Now you can write these filthy words! But what follows?   25
– 'Therefore I hope you will speedily find some way to
free me from this unfortunate match, which was never, I
assure you, of my choice, but I'm afraid 'tis already too
far gone. However, if you love me, as I do you, you will
try what you can do, but you must help me away before   30
tomorrow, or else, alas, I shall be for ever out of your
reach, for I can defer no longer our' – (*The letter*
concludes) 'Our'? What is to follow 'our'? Speak, what?
Our journey into the country I suppose? Oh, woman,
damned woman!   And love, damned love, their old   35
tempter! For this is one of his miracles. In a moment
he can make those blind that could see, and those see
that were blind, those dumb that could speak, and those
prattle who were dumb before; nay, what is more than
all, make these dough-baked, senseless, indocile   40

13 *studied* thought about
    like anything very hard; vulgarism
27 *match*   This usually means an engagement rather than a marriage;
    seems a bit disingenuous.
36–9 paraphrase of Isaiah 35:5–6
40 *dough-baked* half-baked   *indocile* hard to teach

animals, women, too hard for us, their politic lords and rulers, in a moment. But make an end of your letter and then I'll make an end of you thus, and all my plagues together. *Draws his sword*

MRS PINCHWIFE

O Lord, O Lord, you are such a passionate man, bud. 45

Enter SPARKISH

SPARKISH

How now, what's here to do?

PINCHWIFE

This fool here now!

SPARKISH

What, drawn upon your wife? You should never do that, but at night in the dark, when you can't hurt her! This is my sister-in-law, is it not? (*Pulls aside her handkerchief*) 50 Ay, faith, e'en our country Margery; one may know her. Come, she and you must go dine with me; dinner's ready, come. But where's my wife? Is she not come home yet? Where is she?

PINCHWIFE

Making you a cuckold; 'tis that they all do, as soon as 55 they can.

SPARKISH

What, the wedding day? No, a wife that designs to make a cully of her husband will be sure to let him win the first stake of love, by the world. But come, they stay dinner for us. Come, I'll lead down our Margery. 60

PINCHWIFE

No! – Sir, go, we'll follow you.

SPARKISH

I will not wag without you.

PINCHWIFE [*Aside*]

This coxcomb is a sensible torment to me amidst the greatest in the world.

41 *politic* lawful
48 *drawn* both having a sword drawn and ready for sex; play on words
50 sd *handkerchief* head-dress
58 *cully* Q1–4, O (cuckold Q5) dupe, especially cuckold
61 sp PINCHWIFE ed. (*Mrs. Pin.* Q1-5, O)
62 *wag* go
63 *sensible* painful

SPARKISH

Come, come, Madam Margery.   65

PINCHWIFE

No, I'll lead her my way. (*Leads her to t'other door and
locks her in and returns*) What, would you treat your
friends with mine, for want of your own wife? (*Aside*) I
am contented my rage should take breath.

SPARKISH [*Aside*]

I told Horner this.   70

PINCHWIFE

Come now.

SPARKISH

Lord, how shy you are of your wife! But let me tell you,
brother, we men of wit have amongst us a saying that
cuckolding, like the smallpox, comes with a fear, and
you may keep your wife as much as you will out of   75
danger of infection, but if her constitution incline her
to't, she'll have it sooner or later, by the world, say they.

PINCHWIFE (*Aside*)

What a thing is a cuckold, that every fool can make him
ridiculous! – Well sir, but let me advise you, now you
are come to be concerned, because you suspect the   80
danger, not to neglect the means to prevent it, especially
when the greatest share of the malady will light upon
your own head, for –

    Hows'e'er the kind wife's belly comes to swell,

    The husband breeds for her, and first is ill.   85

                                          [*Exeunt*]

Act V, Scene i

PINCHWIFE'*s house*
Enter PINCHWIFE *and* MRS PINCHWIFE
A table and candle

PINCHWIFE

Come, take the pen and make an end of the letter, just
as you intended. If you are false in a tittle, I shall soon
perceive it, and punish you with this as you deserve.

---

65 *Madam Margery* form of address implying high social status; Sparkish at
   his most ceremonious
72 *how shy you are of* how cautious you are about
74 *comes with a fear* is brought on by fearing it
85 *breeds for her* grows cuckold's horns on her behalf

(*Lays his hand on his sword*) Write what was to follow –   5
let's see – 'You must make haste and help me away
before tomorrow, or else I shall be for ever out of your
reach, for I can defer no longer our' – What follows
'our'?

MRS PINCHWIFE

Must all out then, bud? (MRS PINCHWIFE *takes the pen
and writes*) Look you there, then.   10

PINCHWIFE

Let's see – 'For I can defer no longer our wedding.
Your slighted Alithea'. – What's the meaning of this?
My sister's name to't? Speak, unriddle!

MRS PINCHWIFE

Yes, indeed, bud.

PINCHWIFE

But why her name to't? Speak – speak I say!   15

MRS PINCHWIFE

Ay, but you'll tell her then again. If you would not tell
her again –

PINCHWIFE

I will not; I am stunned; my head turns round. Speak!

MRS PINCHWIFE

Won't you tell her indeed, and indeed?

PINCHWIFE

No, speak I say.   20

MRS PINCHWIFE

She'll be angry with me, but I had rather she should be
angry with me than you, bud. And to tell you the truth
'twas she made me write the letter, and taught me what
I should write.

PINCHWIFE

Ha! (*Aside*) I thought the style was somewhat better   25
than her own. – But how could she come to you to
teach you, since I had locked you up alone?

MRS PINCHWIFE

Oh, through the keyhole, bud.

PINCHWIFE

But why should she make you write a letter for her to
him, since she can write herself?   30

MRS PINCHWIFE

Why, she said because – for I was unwilling to do it.

16 *tell her then again* repeat it to her
25 sd (*Aside*) Q4–5, O (Q1–3 *omit*)
26 *but how* Q1–3 (Q4–5, O *omit*)

PINCHWIFE
Because what – because?

MRS PINCHWIFE
Because, lest Master Horner should be cruel and refuse
her, or vain afterwards, and show the letter, she might
disown it, the hand not being hers.   35

PINCHWIFE (*Aside*)
How's this? Ha – then I think I shall come to myself
again. This changeling could not invent this lie, but if
she could, why should she? She might think I should
soon discover it – stay – now I think on't too, Horner
said he was sorry she had married Sparkish, and her   40
disowning her marriage to me makes me think she has
evaded it for Horner's sake. Yet why should she take
this course? But men in love are fools; women may well
be so. – But hark you, madam, your sister went out in
the morning and I have not seen her within since.   45

MRS PINCHWIFE
Alackaday, she has been crying all day above, it seems,
in a corner.

PINCHWIFE
Where is she? Let me speak with her.

MRS PINCHWIFE (*Aside*)
O Lord, then he'll discover all! – Pray hold, bud. What,
d'ye mean to discover me? She'll know I have told you 50
then. Pray bud, let me talk with her first.

PINCHWIFE
I must speak with her to know whether Horner ever
made her any promise; and whether she be married to
Sparkish or no.

MRS PINCHWIFE
Pray, dear bud, don't, till I have spoken with her and 55
told her that I have told you all, for she'll kill me else.

PINCHWIFE
Go then, and bid her come out to me.

MRS PINCHWIFE
Yes, yes, bud.

PINCHWIFE
Let me see –

MRS PINCHWIFE [*Aside*]
I'll go, but she is not within to come to him. I have just 60
got time to know of Lucy her maid, who first set me on

38 *might* would surely
50 *discover* betray

work, what lie I shall tell next, for I am e'en at my wit's
end!

Exit MRS PINCHWIFE

PINCHWIFE
Well, I resolve it; Horner shall have her. I'd rather give
him my sister than lend him my wife, and such an   65
alliance will prevent his pretensions to my wife, sure. I'll
make him of kin to her, and then he won't care for her.

MRS PINCHWIFE returns

MRS PINCHWIFE
O Lord, bud, I told you what anger you would make me
with my sister.
PINCHWIFE
Won't she come hither?   70
MRS PINCHWIFE
No, no, alackaday, she's ashamed to look you in the
face, and she says if you go in to her, she'll run away
downstairs, and shamefully go herself to Master Horner,
who has promised her marriage, she says, and she will
have no other, so she won't.   75
PINCHWIFE
Did he so – promise her marriage? Then she shall have
no other. Go tell her so, and if she will come and
discourse with me a little concerning the means, I will
about it immediately. Go!

(Exit MRS PINCHWIFE)

His estate is equal to Sparkish's, and his extraction as   80
much better than his as his parts are. But my chief
reason is, I'd rather be of kin to him by the name of
brother-in-law than that of cuckold.

Enter MRS PINCHWIFE

Well, what says she now?
MRS PINCHWIFE
Why, she says she would only have you lead her to   85
Horner's lodging – with whom she first will discourse
the matter before she talk with you, which yet she

---

81 *parts* abilities. A deliberate pun on private parts is possible, as
    Pinchwife does not suppose Horner a eunuch, but it is not probable, as
    the word has no suggestive context and is not repeated. Compare
    II.i.276–7.
87 *talk* Q1–3 (talks Q4–5, O). Perhaps Mrs Pinchwife's grammar should be
    preserved.

cannot do. For alack, poor creature, she says she can't
so much as look you in the face, therefore she'll come to
you in a mask. And you must excuse her if she make   90
you no answer to any question of yours till you have
brought her to Master Horner. And if you will not chide
her nor question her she'll come out to you immediately.

PINCHWIFE

Let her come. I will not speak a word to her, nor require
a word from her.   95

MRS PINCHWIFE

Oh, I forgot – besides, she says, she cannot look you in
the face, though through a mask, therefore would desire
you to put out the candle.

PINCHWIFE

I agree to all; let her make haste.

                              (*Exit* MRS PINCHWIFE)
There 'tis out.   (*Puts out the candle*)   My case is 100
something better; I'd rather fight with Horner for not
lying with my sister than for lying with my wife, and of
the two I had rather find my sister too forward than my
wife. I expected no other from her free education, as
she calls it, and her passion for the town. Well, wife and 105
sister are names which make us expect love and duty,
pleasure and comfort, but we find 'em plagues and
torments,   and   are   equally,   though   differently
troublesome to their keeper; for we have as much ado to
get people to lie with our sisters as to keep 'em from 110
lying with our wives.

Enter MRS PINCHWIFE *masked, and in hoods and scarves,
and a night gown and petticoat of* ALITHEA's,
in the dark

What, are you come, sister? Let us go then – but first let
me lock up my wife. Mistress Margery, where are you?

MRS PINCHWIFE

Here, bud.

---

100 sd *puts out the candle* This makes the stage symbolically dark, so that he
        cannot see his wife is disguised as Alithea, but the audience can.
101–2 *not lying with* refusing to marry.   Pinchwife uses the same gross
        idiom at I.i.368.
111 sd *scarves* ornamental strips of silk
        night gown loose gown or wrap, not necessarily worn only indoors
        petticoat skirt

PINCHWIFE

Come hither, that I may lock you up. (MRS PINCHWIFE 115
gives him her hand, but when he lets her go, she steals softly
on t'other side of him) Get you in. (*Locks the door*)
Come, sister, where are you now?

[MRS PINCHWIFE] *is led away by him for his sister Alithea*

[Act V, Scene ii]

The scene changes to HORNER*'s lodging*
QUACK, HORNER

QUACK

What, all alone? Not so much as one of your cuckolds
here, nor one of their wives! They use to take their turns
with you, as if they were to watch you.

HORNER

Yes, it often happens that a cuckold is but his wife's spy,
and is more upon family duty when he is with her gallant   5
abroad, hindering his pleasure, than when he is at home
with her, playing the gallant. But the hardest duty a
married woman imposes upon a lover is keeping her
husband company always.

QUACK

And his fondness wearies you almost as soon as hers.   10

HORNER

A pox! keeping a cuckold company after you have had
his wife is as tiresome as the company of a country
squire to a witty fellow of the town, when he has got all
his money.

QUACK

And as at first a man makes a friend of the husband to   15
get the wife, so at last you are fain to fall out with the
wife to be rid of the husband.

HORNER

Ay, most cuckold-makers are true courtiers. When once
a poor man has cracked his credit for 'em, they can't
abide to come near him.   20

---

118 sd *for* in mistake for
  2 *use to* are accustomed to
  5 *more upon family duty* doing more for family honour
 19 *cracked his credit* (literally) bankrupted himself;   (metaphorically)
     become a cuckold

QUACK

But at first, to draw him in, are so sweet, so kind, so
dear, just as you are to Pinchwife. But what becomes of
that intrigue with his wife?

HORNER

A pox! He's as surly as an alderman that has been bit,
and since he's so coy, his wife's kindness is in vain, for   25
she's a silly innocent.

QUACK

Did she not send you a letter by him?

HORNER

Yes, but that's a riddle I have not yet solved. Allow the
poor creature to be willing, she is silly too, and he keeps
her up so close –   30

QUACK

Yes, so close that he makes her but the more willing,
and adds but revenge to her love, which two, when met,
seldom fail of satisfying each other one way or other.

HORNER

What! here's the man we are talking of, I think.

Enter PINCHWIFE *leading in his wife, masked, muffled,
and in her sister's gown*

Pshaw!   35

QUACK

Bringing his wife to you is the next thing to bringing a
love letter from her.

HORNER

What means this?

PINCHWIFE

The last time, you know, sir, I brought you a love letter.
Now you see a mistress. I think you'll say I am a civil   40
man to you.

HORNER

Ay, the devil take me, will I say thou art the civillest man
I ever met with, and I have known some. I fancy I
understand thee now better than I did the letter. But
hark thee, in thy ear –   45

PINCHWIFE

What?

24   *bit* tricked
25   *coy* cautious
      kindness readiness for sex. See also III.ii.540.

HORNER

Nothing but the usual question, man; is she sound, on thy word?

PINCHWIFE

What, you take her for a wench, and me for a pimp?

HORNER

Pshaw! wench and pimp, paw words. I know thou art   50
an honest fellow, and hast a great acquaintance amongst
the ladies, and perhaps hast made love for me rather
than let me make love to thy wife –

PINCHWIFE

Come sir; in short, I am for no fooling.

HORNER

Nor I neither;   therefore prithee let's see her face   55
presently. Make her show, man! Art thou sure I don't
know her?

PINCHWIFE

I am sure you do know her.

HORNER

A pox! why dost thou bring her to me then?

PINCHWIFE

Because she's a relation of mine –   60

HORNER

Is she, faith, man? Then thou art still more civil and
obliging, dear rogue.

PINCHWIFE

– who desired me to bring her to you.

HORNER

Then she is obliging, dear rogue.

PINCHWIFE

You'll make her welcome, for my sake, I hope.   65

HORNER

I hope she is handsome enough to make herself
welcome. Prithee, let her unmask.

PINCHWIFE

Do you speak to her. She would never be ruled by me.

HORNER

Madam – (MRS PINCHWIFE *whispers to* HORNER) She says
she must speak with me in private. Withdraw, prithee.   70

47 *sound* free from pox
50 *paw* improper, naughty, or obscene (*OED*)
56 *show* show herself
69–91 Q1–5, O substantially agree in their stage directions, but the stage
    business is not obvious. I think Mrs Pinchwife and Horner detach

PINCHWIFE (*Aside*)

She's unwilling, it seems, I should know all her undecent conduct in this business. – Well, then, I'll leave you together, and hope when I am gone you'll agree. If not, you and I shan't agree, sir.

HORNER [*Aside*]

What means the fool? – If she and I agree, 'tis no matter   75
what you and I do.

> *Whispers to* MRS PINCHWIFE *who makes signs*
> *with her hand for him to be gone*

PINCHWIFE [*Aside*]

In the meantime I'll fetch a parson, and find out Sparkish and disabuse him. – You would have me fetch a parson, would you not? Well, then – [*Aside*] Now I think I am rid of her, and shall have no more trouble   80
with her.   Our sisters and daughters, like usurers' money, are safest when put out, but our wives, like their writings, never safe but in our closets under lock and key.

Exit PINCHWIFE

Enter BOY

BOY

Sir Jaspar Fidget, sir, is coming up.   85

[*Exit* BOY]

HORNER [*Aside to* QUACK]

Here's the trouble of a cuckold, now, we are talking of. A pox on him! Has he not enough to do to hinder his wife's sport, but he must other women's too? – Step in here madam.

Exit MRS PINCHWIFE

Enter SIR JASPAR

---

themselves from Pinchwife and whisper together; Pinchwife addresses himself partly to the audience and partly to them. Horner after his aside at l. 75 speaks to Pinchwife and then whispers to Mrs Pinchwife, who makes signs for 'him' (i.e., Pinchwife) to   be gone throughout Pinchwife's exit speech. After the boy has announced Sir Jaspar Fidget, Horner addresses first Quack and then Mrs Pinchwife, who is hustled into the bedroom.

76   sd *hand* Q1-4, O (*hands* Q5)
82   *put out* invested
82-3   *their writings* the usurers' documents
86   *are* were; historic present. They were talking of Sir Jaspar in ll. 1–22.

SIR JASPAR

My best and dearest friend.   90

HORNER [*Aside to* QUACK]

The old style, doctor. – Well, be short, for I am busy. What would your impertinent wife have now?

SIR JASPAR

Well guessed, i'faith, for I do come from her.

HORNER

To invite me to supper? Tell her I can't come. Go.

SIR JASPAR

Nay, now you are out, faith, for my lady and the whole   95
knot of the virtuous gang, as they call themselves, are resolved upon a frolic of coming to you tonight in a masquerade, and are all dressed already.

HORNER

I shan't be at home.

SIR JASPAR (*Aside*)

Lord, how churlish he is to women! – Nay, prithee   100
don't disappoint 'em, they'll think 'tis my fault, prithee don't. I'll send in the banquet and the fiddles. But make no noise on't, for the poor virtuous rogues would not have it known for the world, that they go a-masquerading, and they would come to no man's ball   105
but yours.

HORNER

Well, well – get you gone, and tell 'em, if they come, 'twill be at the peril of their honour and yours.

SIR JASPAR

He, he, he! We'll trust you for that, farewell.

Exit SIR JASPAR

HORNER

Doctor, anon, you too shall be my guest,   110
But now I'm going to a private feast.

[*Exeunt*]

---

91   *the old style* the sort of address we would expect
96   *gang* society; not as colloquial and pejorative a word as it is now
97–8   *a masquerade* Q1-3 (masquerade Q4-5, O)
102   *banquet* refreshments
        fiddles fiddlers, as at II.i.82. Possibly Sir Jaspar's musicians play for the dance of cuckolds at the end of V.iv.
105   *ball* party, as at II.i.82

[Act V, Scene iii]

The scene changes to the Piazza of Covent Garden
SPARKISH, PINCHWIFE

SPARKISH (*With the letter in his hand*)
But who would have thought a woman could have been
false to me? By the world, I could not have thought it.
PINCHWIFE
You were for giving and taking liberty; she has taken it
only, sir, now you find in that letter. You are a frank
person, and so is she, you see there.   5
SPARKISH
Nay, if this be her hand – for I never saw it.
PINCHWIFE
'Tis no matter whether that be her hand or no. I am
sure this hand, at her desire, led her to Master Horner,
with whom I left her just now, to go fetch a parson to
'em, at their desire too, to deprive you of her for ever,   10
for it seems yours was but a mock marriage.
SPARKISH
Indeed, she would needs have it that 'twas Harcourt
himself in a parson's habit that married us, but I'm sure
he told me 'twas his brother Ned.
PINCHWIFE
Oh, there 'tis out, and you were deceived, not she, for   15
you are such a frank person – but I must be gone. You'll
find her at Master Horner's. Go and believe your eyes.
                                                    Exit PINCHWIFE
SPARKISH
Nay, I'll to her, and call her as many crocodiles, sirens,
harpies, and other heathenish names as a poet would do
a mistress who had refused to hear his suit, nay more,   20
his verses on her. But stay, is not that she following a
torch at t'other end of the Piazza? And from Horner's
certainly – 'tis so.

Enter ALITHEA *following a torch, and* LUCY *behind*

You are well met, madam, though you don't think so.

1 sd *the letter* i.e., that written by Mrs Pinchwife. Pinchwife has now
   told Sparkish it was written by Alithea.
4 *frank* generous. See III.ii.360.
6 *hand* handwriting
18 *crocodiles* hypocrites
22 *torch* linkboy with torch

What, you have made a short visit to Master Horner,   25
but I suppose you'll return to him presently. By that
time the parson can be with him.

ALITHEA

Master Horner, and the parson, sir?

SPARKISH

Come, madam, no more dissembling, no more jilting,
for I am no more a frank person.   30

ALITHEA

How's this?

LUCY (*Aside*)

So, 'twill work, I see.

SPARKISH

Could you find out no easy country fool to abuse?
None but me, a gentleman of wit and pleasure about the
town? But it was your pride to be too hard for a man of   35
parts, unworthy false woman! False as a friend that
lends a man money to lose. False as dice, who undo
those that trust all they have to 'em.

LUCY (*Aside*)

He has been a great bubble by his similes, as they say.

ALITHEA

You have been too merry, sir, at your wedding dinner,   40
sure.

SPARKISH

What, d'ye mock me too?

ALITHEA

Or you have been deluded.

SPARKISH

By you!

ALITHEA

Let me understand you.   45

SPARKISH

Have you the confidence – I should call it something
else, since you know your guilt – to stand my just
reproaches? You did not write an impudent letter to
Master Horner, who I find now has clubbed with you in
deluding me with his aversion for women, that I might   50
not, forsooth, suspect him for my rival?

LUCY (*Aside*)

D'ye think the gentleman can be jealous now, madam?

29 *jilting* deceiving
39 Judging by his similes, he has been tricked many times, as they say.

ALITHEA

I write a letter to Master Horner!

SPARKISH

Nay, madam, do not deny it. Your brother showed it
me just now, and told me likewise he left you at   55
Horner's lodging to fetch a parson to marry you to him.
And I wish you joy, madam, joy, joy! and to him, too,
much joy! and to myself more joy for not marrying you!

ALITHEA (*Aside*)

So I find my brother would break off the match, and I
can consent to't, since I see this gentleman can be made   60
jealous. – O Lucy, by his rude usage and jealousy, he
makes me almost afraid I am married to him. Art thou
sure 'twas Harcourt himself and no parson that married
us?

SPARKISH

No, madam, I thank you.   I suppose that was a   65
contrivance too of Master Horner's and yours, to make
Harcourt play the parson. But I would, as little as you,
have him one now, no, not for the world, for shall I tell
you another truth? I never had any passion for you till
now, for now I hate you. 'Tis true I might have married   70
your portion, as other men of parts of the town do
sometimes; and so your servant.   And to show my
unconcernedness, I'll come to your wedding and resign
you with as much joy as I would a stale wench to a new
cully. Nay, with as much joy as I would after the first   75
night, if I had been married to you. There's for you, and
so your servant, servant.

Exit SPARKISH

ALITHEA

How was I deceived in a man!

LUCY

You'll believe, then, a fool may be made jealous now?
For that easiness in him that suffers him to be led by a   80
wife, will likewise permit him to be persuaded against
her by others.

ALITHEA

But marry Master Horner! My brother does not intend
it, sure. If I thought he did, I would take thy advice and
Master Harcourt for my husband. And now I wish that   85

---

72 *and so your servant* He takes leave, but has afterthoughts.

76–7 *and so your servant, servant* He takes leave again, but adds a mocking
quibble on 'servant' in the sense of lover.

if there be any over-wise woman of the town, who, like
me, would marry a fool for fortune, liberty, or title: first,
that her husband may love play, and be a cully to all the
town, but her, and suffer none but fortune to be mistress
of his purse. Then, if for liberty, that he may send her   90
into the country under the conduct of some housewifely
mother-in-law. And, if for title, may the world give 'em
none but that of cuckold.

LUCY

And for her greater curse, madam, may he not deserve
it.   95

ALITHEA

Away, impertinent!   – Is not this my Old Lady
Lanterlu's?

LUCY

Yes, madam. (*Aside*) And here I hope we shall find
Master Harcourt.

Exeunt ALITHEA, LUCY

[Act V, Scene iv]

The scene changes again to HORNER*'s lodging*
HORNER, LADY FIDGET, *Mrs* DAINTY FIDGET, *Mrs*
SQUEAMISH. *A table, banquet and bottles*

HORNER (*Aside*)

A pox! they are come too soon – before I have sent back
my new – mistress. All I have now to do is to lock her
in, that they may not see her.

LADY FIDGET

That we may be sure of our welcome, we have brought
our entertainment with us, and are resolved to treat   5
thee, dear toad.

DAINTY

And that we may be merry to purpose, have left Sir
Jaspar and my old Lady Squeamish quarrelling at home
at backgammon.

SQUEAMISH

Therefore, let us make use of our time, lest they should   10
chance to interrupt us.

---

97 *Lanterlu's* from lanterloo or loo, a popular card game. See Epilogue,
    l. 27.
 2 *new – mistress* He had been going to use some other word.

LADY FIDGET
 Let us sit then.
HORNER
 First, that you may be private, let me lock this door and
 that, and I'll wait upon you presently.
LADY FIDGET
 No, sir, shut 'em only and your lips for ever, for we must 15
 trust you as much as our women.
HORNER
 You know all vanity's killed in me; I have no occasion
 for talking.
LADY FIDGET
 Now, ladies, supposing we had drank each of us our two
 bottles, let us speak the truth of our hearts. 20
DAINTY *and* SQUEAMISH
 Agreed.
LADY FIDGET
 By this brimmer, for truth is nowhere else to be found.
 (*Aside* to HORNER) Not in thy heart, false man!
HORNER (*Aside to* LADY FIDGET)
 You have found me a true man, I'm sure!
LADY FIDGET (*Aside to* HORNER)
 Not every way. – But let us sit and be merry. 25

LADY FIDGET sings

1.

 Why should our damned tyrants oblige us to live
 On the pittance of pleasure which they only give?
   We must not rejoice
   With wine and with noise.
 In vain we must wake in a dull bed alone, 30
 Whilst to our warm rival, the bottle, they're gone.
   Then lay aside charms
   And take up these arms.

2.

 'Tis wine only gives 'em their courage and wit
 Because we live sober, to men we submit. 35
   If for beauties you'd pass
   Take a lick of the glass:
 'Twill mend your complexions, and when they are gone

---

22 *brimmer* full glass
25 sd The music for this song is lost.
33 *arms* glasses, as explained by a marginal gloss in Q1–5, O

> The best red we have is the red of the grape.
> > Then, sisters, lay't on,   40
> > And damn a good shape.

DAINTY

Dear brimmer! Well, in token of our openness and plain-dealing, let us throw our masks over our heads.

HORNER

So, 'twill come to the glasses anon.

SQUEAMISH

Lovely brimmer! Let me enjoy him first.   45

LADY FIDGET

No, I never part with a gallant till I've tried him. Dear brimmer, that mak'st our husbands short-sighted.

DAINTY

And our bashful gallants bold.

SQUEAMISH

And for want of a gallant, the butler lovely in our eyes. Drink, eunuch.   50

LADY FIDGET

Drink thou representative of a husband. Damn a husband!

DAINTY

And, as it were a husband, an old keeper.

SQUEAMISH

And an old grandmother.

HORNER

And an English bawd, and a French surgeon.   55

LADY FIDGET

Ay, we have all reason to curse 'em.

HORNER

For my sake, ladies?

LADY FIDGET

No, for our own, for the first spoils all young gallants' industry.

DAINTY

And the other's art makes 'em bold only with common   60 women.

SQUEAMISH

And rather run the hazard of the vile distemper amongst them, than of a denial amongst us.

---

39   *red* rouge   41   *shape* figure

45   *him* This and Lady Fidget's response suggest *brimmer* should be a *double entendre*. Partridge and others record *brim sb.* 'harlot' and *v.* 'to have intercourse'.

DAINTY

The filthy toads choose mistresses now as they do stuffs,
for having been fancied and worn by others.   65

SQUEAMISH

For being common and cheap.

LADY FIDGET

Whilst women of quality, like the richest stuffs, lie
untumbled and unasked for.

HORNER

Ay, neat, and cheap, and new, often they think best.

DAINTY

No, sir, the beasts will be known by a mistress longer   70
than by a suit.

SQUEAMISH

And 'tis not for cheapness neither.

LADY FIDGET

No, for the vain fops will take up druggets and
embroider 'em. But I wonder at the depraved appetites
of witty men; they use to be out of the common road   75
and hate imitation. Pray tell me, beast, when you were
a man, why you rather chose to club with a multitude in
a common house for an entertainment than to be the
only guest at a good table?

HORNER

Why, faith, ceremony and expectation are unsufferable   80
to those that are sharp bent. People always eat with
the best stomach at an ordinary, where every man is
snatching for the best bit.

LADY FIDGET

Though he get a cut over the fingers. But I have heard
people eat most heartily of another man's meat, that is,   85
what they do not pay for.

---

64 *stuffs* cloth
68 *untumbled* (of cloth) unhandled; (of women) unwanted for sex; 'Before
    you tumbled me, / You promised me to wed' (*Hamlet* IV.v.62–3)
73 *druggets* cheap wool fabrics
75 *use to be* are usually
78 *common house* restaurant or perhaps brothel
80 *expectation* waiting
81 *are sharp bent* have a keen appetite
82 *ordinary* restaurant
84 *cut over the fingers* probably alluding to Horner's supposed surgical
    disaster

HORNER

When they are sure of their welcome and freedom, for
ceremony in love and eating is as ridiculous as in
fighting. Falling on briskly is all should be done in
those occasions.   90

LADY FIDGET

Well then, let me tell you, sir, there is nowhere more
freedom than in our houses, and we take freedom from a
young person as a sign of good breeding, and a person
may be as free as he pleases with us, as frolic, as
gamesome, as wild as he will.   95

HORNER

Ha'n't I heard you all declaim against wild men?

LADY FIDGET

Yes, but for all that, we think wildness in a man as
desirable a quality as in a duck or rabbit. A tame man,
foh!

HORNER

I know not, but your reputations frightened me, as much   100
as your faces invited me.

LADY FIDGET

Our reputation! Lord, why should you not think that we
women make use of our reputation, as you men of
yours, only to deceive the world with less suspicion?
Our virtue is like the statesman's religion, the Quaker's   105
word, the gamester's oath, and the great man's honour –
but to cheat those that trust us.

SQUEAMISH

And that demureness, coyness, and modesty that you
see in our faces in the boxes at plays is as much a sign of
a kind woman as a vizard-mask in the pit.   110

DAINTY

For, I assure you, women are least masked when they
have the velvet vizard on.

LADY FIDGET

You would have found us modest women in our denials
only.

---

89 *falling on* (in love) having sex, (in eating) starting, (in fighting) attacking
96 *wild* See Etherege's *She Would if she Could* (ed. Charlene M. Taylor)
I.ii.37–9: 'There is not such another wild man in the Town. All his talk
was of wenching, and swearing, and drinking, and tearing'.
110 *kind* available for sex
vizard-mask sign of a whore. See I.i.186 note.

SQUEAMISH

Our bashfulness is only the reflection of the men's.   115

DAINTY

We blush, when they are shamefaced.

HORNER

I beg your pardon, ladies.   I was deceived in you
devilishly. But why that mighty pretence to honour?

LADY FIDGET

We have told you.   But sometimes 'twas for the same
reason you men pretend business often, to avoid ill 120
company, to enjoy the better and more privately those
you love.

HORNER

But why would you ne'er give a friend a wink then?

LADY FIDGET

Faith, your reputation frightened us as much as ours did
you, you were so notoriously lewd.   125

HORNER

And you so seemingly honest.

LADY FIDGET

Was that all that deterred you?

HORNER

And so expensive – you allow freedom, you say? –

LADY FIDGET

Ay, ay.

HORNER

– that I was afraid of losing my little money, as well as 130
my little time, both which my other pleasures required.

LADY FIDGET

Money, foh! You talk like a little fellow now. Do such
as we expect money?

HORNER

I beg your pardon, madam. I must confess, I have heard
that great ladies, like great merchants, set but the higher 135
prices upon what they have, because they are not in
necessity of taking the first offer.

DAINTY

Such as we, make sale of our hearts?

SQUEAMISH

We bribed for our love? Foh!

HORNER

With your pardon, ladies, I know, like great men in 140

126 *honest* chaste
128 *freedom* plain-dealing

offices, you seem to exact flattery and attendance only
from your followers, but you have receivers about you,
and such fees to pay, a man is afraid to pass your grants.
Besides, we must let you win at cards, or we lose your
hearts.   And if you make an assignation, 'tis at a 145
goldsmith's, jeweller's, or china house, where, for your
honour you deposit to him, he must pawn his to the
punctual cit, and so paying for what you take up, pays
for what he takes up.

DAINTY
Would you not have us assured of our gallant's love?   150

SQUEAMISH
For love is better known by liberality than by jealousy.

LADY FIDGET
For one may be dissembled, the other not. (*Aside*) But
my jealousy can be no longer dissembled, and they are
telling ripe. – Come, here's to our gallants in waiting,
whom we must name, and I'll begin. This is my false 155
rogue.   *Claps him on the back*

SQUEAMISH
How!

HORNER [*Aside*]
So, all will out now.

SQUEAMISH (*Aside to* HORNER)
Did you not tell me, 'twas for my sake only you reported
yourself no man?   160

DAINTY (*Aside to* HORNER)
Oh wretch! Did you not swear to me, 'twas for my love
and honour you passed for that thing you do?

HORNER
So, so.

LADY FIDGET
Come, speak ladies; this is my false villain.

SQUEAMISH
And mine too.   165

---

142   *receivers* servants who take bribes
143   *pass your grants* accept your favours
146–8 *for your honour ... punctual cit* for trusting your honour to him, he must
          pawn his to the punctilious shopkeeper
153–4 *jealousy* Q1-2 4-5, O (jealousies Q3); *they are telling ripe* they (the other
          ladies) are ready to be told. But if Q3 is right, the phrase means they
          (the jealousies) are ready to be told, i.e. very strong.
154   *gallants in waiting* lovers awaiting our pleasure; phrase coined on the
          analogy of ladies in waiting

DAINTY

And mine.

HORNER

Well, then, you are all three my false rogues too, and
there's an end on't.

LADY FIDGET

Well, then, there's no remedy; sister sharers, let us not
fall out, but have a care of our honour. Though we get 170
no presents, no jewels of him, we are savers of our
honour, the jewel of most value and use, which shines
yet to the world unsuspected, though it be counterfeit.

HORNER

Nay, and is e'en as good as if it were true, provided the
world think so; for honour, like beauty, now, only 175
depends on the opinion of others.

LADY FIDGET

Well, Harry Common, I hope you can be true to three.
Swear – but 'tis no purpose to require your oath; for
you are as often forsworn as you swear to new women.

HORNER

Come, faith, madam, let us e'en pardon one another, for 180
all the difference I find betwixt we men and you women,
we forswear ourselves at the beginning of an amour, you
as long as it lasts.

Enter SIR JASPAR FIDGET *and* OLD LADY SQUEAMISH

SIR JASPAR

Oh, my Lady Fidget, was this your cunning to come to
Master Horner without me? But you have been 185
nowhere else, I hope.

LADY FIDGET

No, Sir Jaspar.

OLD LADY SQUEAMISH

And you came straight hither, Biddy?

SQUEAMISH

Yes, indeed, lady grandmother.

SIR JASPAR

'Tis well, 'tis well. I knew when once they were 190
thoroughly acquainted with poor Horner they'd ne'er be
from him. You may let her masquerade it with my wife
and Horner, and I warrant her reputation safe.

---

177 *Harry Common* a womaniser or perhaps a stud; on the analogy of Doll
Common, the prostitute in *The Alchemist*

Enter BOY

BOY

Oh, sir, here's the gentleman come whom you bid me
not suffer to come up without giving you notice, with a 195
lady, too, and other gentlemen.

HORNER

Do you all go in there, whilst I send 'em away, and boy,
do you desire 'em to stay below till I come, which shall
be immediately.

Exeunt SIR JASPAR, LADY SQUEAMISH, LADY FIDGET,
Mrs DAINTY, SQUEAMISH

BOY

Yes, sir.   *Exit* 200

Exit HORNER *at t'other door, and returns with*
MRS PINCHWIFE

HORNER

You would not take my advice to be gone home before
your husband came back; he'll now discover all. Yet
pray, my dearest, be persuaded to go home, and leave
the rest to my management. I'll let you down the back
way.   205

MRS PINCHWIFE

I don't know the way home, so I don't.

HORNER

My man shall wait upon you.

MRS PINCHWIFE

No, don't you believe that I'll go at all. What, are you
weary of me already?

HORNER

No, my life, 'tis that I may love you long, 'tis to secure 210
my love, and your reputation with your husband. He'll
never receive you again else.

MRS PINCHWIFE

What care I? D'ye think to frighten me with that? I
don't intend to go to him again. You shall be my
husband now.   215

HORNER

I cannot be your husband, dearest, since you are
married to him.

MRS PINCHWIFE

Oh, would you make me believe that? Don't I see every
day at London here, women leave their first husbands,
and go and live with other men as their wives? Pish, 220

pshaw! You'd make me angry, but that I love you so
mainly.

HORNER

So, they are coming up. – In again, in, I hear 'em.

(*Exit* MRS PINCHWIFE)

Well, a silly mistress is like a weak place, soon got, soon
lost; a man has scarce time for plunder. She betrays her 225
husband first to her gallant, and then her gallant to her
husband.

Enter PINCHWIFE, ALITHEA, HARCOURT, SPARKISH,
LUCY *and a* PARSON

PINCHWIFE

Come, madam, 'tis not the sudden change of your dress,
the confidence of your asseverations, and your false
witness there, shall persuade me I did not bring you 230
hither just now. Here's my witness, who cannot deny it,
since you must be confronted. – Master Horner, did not
I bring this lady to you just now?

HORNER (*Aside*)

Now must I wrong one woman for another's sake. But
that's no new thing with me; for in these cases I am still 235
on the criminal's side, against the innocent.

ALITHEA

Pray speak, sir.

HORNER (*Aside*)

It must be so. I must be impudent and try my luck;
impudence uses to be too hard for truth.

PINCHWIFE

What, you are studying an evasion, or excuse for her? 240
Speak, sir.

HORNER

No, faith, I am something backward only to speak in
women's affairs or disputes.

PINCHWIFE

She bids you speak.

ALITHEA

Ay, pray sir do, pray satisfy him.   245

HORNER

Then truly, you did bring that lady to me just now.

222 *mainly* strongly
224 *weak place* ill-defended fortress
230 *witness* i.e., Lucy
239 *uses to be* is usually

PINCHWIFE
  O ho!
ALITHEA
  How, sir!
HARCOURT
  How, Horner!
ALITHEA
  What mean you, sir? I always took you for a man of 250
  honour.
HORNER (*Aside*)
  Ay, so much a man of honour that I must save my
  mistress, I thank you, come what will on't.
SPARKISH
  So, if I had had her, she'd have made me believe the
  moon had been made of a Christmas pie.   255
LUCY (*Aside*)
  Now could I speak, if I durst, and solve the riddle, who
  am I the author of it.
ALITHEA
  O unfortunate woman! A combination against my
  honour, which most concerns me now, because you
  share in my disgrace, sir, and it is your censure which I 260
  must now suffer that troubles me, not theirs.
HARCOURT
  Madam, then have no trouble, you shall now see 'tis
  possible for me to love too, without being jealous. I will
  not only believe your innocence myself, but make all the
  world believe it. (*Apart to* HORNER) Horner, I must now 265
  be concerned for this lady's honour.
HORNER
  And I must be concerned for a lady's honour too.
HARCOURT
  This lady has her honour, and I will protect it.
HORNER
  My lady has not her honour, but has given it me to keep,
  and I will preserve it.   270
HARCOURT
  I understand you not.

254–5 *the moon … Christmas pie* i.e., something incredible; usually, that the
    moon is made of green cheese. Perhaps this variant is suggested by
    Horner's name, as Little Jack Horner in the nursery rhyme ate a
    Christmas pie.
256 *solve* Q2–5, O ('solve Q1)
258 *combination* plot

HORNER

I would not have you.

MRS PINCHWIFE (*Peeping in behind*)

What's the matter with 'em all?

PINCHWIFE

Come, come, Master Horner, no more disputing. Here's
the parson; I brought him not in vain.   275

HARCOURT

No, sir, I'll employ him, if this lady please.

PINCHWIFE

How! What d'ye mean?

SPARKISH

Ay, what does he mean?

HORNER

Why, I have resigned your sister to him; he has my
consent.   280

PINCHWIFE

But he has not mine, sir. A woman's injured honour, no
more than a man's can be repaired or satisfied by any
but him that first wronged it. And you shall marry her
presently, or –   *Lays his hand on his sword*

Enter to them MRS PINCHWIFE

MRS PINCHWIFE

O Lord, they'll kill poor Master Horner! Besides he   285
shan't marry her whilst I stand by and look on. I'll not
lose my second husband so.

PINCHWIFE

What do I see?

ALITHEA

My sister in my clothes!

SPARKISH

Ha!   290

MRS PINCHWIFE

Nay, pray now don't quarrel about finding work for the
parson. He shall marry me to Master Horner. (*To*
PINCHWIFE) For now I believe you have enough of me.

HORNER

Damned, damned loving changeling!

MRS PINCHWIFE

Pray, sister, pardon me for telling so many lies of you.   295

---

276 sp *HARCOURT* Q5 (*Hor.* Q1-4, O). This speech suits Harcourt rather
than Horner, who has no intention of marrying Alithea, as his speech at
1. 279 shows. An easy printer's error.

HARCOURT

I suppose the riddle is plain now.

LUCY

No, that must be my work. Good sir, hear me.

Kneels to PINCHWIFE, *who stands doggedly,*
with his hat over his eyes

PINCHWIFE

I will never hear woman again, but make 'em all silent,
thus –   *Offers to draw upon his wife*

HORNER

No, that must not be.   300

PINCHWIFE

You then shall go first, 'tis all one to me.

Offers to draw on HORNER; *stopped by* HARCOURT

HARCOURT

Hold!

Enter SIR JASPAR FIDGET, LADY FIDGET, LADY SQUEAMISH,
Mrs DAINTY FIDGET, *Mrs* SQUEAMISH

SIR JASPAR

What's the matter? what's the matter? pray, what's the
matter, sir? I beseech you communicate, sir.

PINCHWIFE

Why, my wife has communicated, sir, as your wife may 305
have done too, sir, if she knows him, sir.

SIR JASPAR

Pshaw! with him! ha, ha, he!

PINCHWIFE

D'ye mock me, sir? A cuckold is a kind of a wild beast,
have a care, sir!

SIR JASPAR

No, sure, you mock me, sir. He cuckold you! It can't 310
be, ha, ha, he! Why, I'll tell you, sir –   *Offers to whisper*

PINCHWIFE

I tell you again, he has whored my wife, and yours too, if
he knows her, and all the women he comes near. 'Tis
not his dissembling, his hypocrisy, can wheedle me.

SIR JASPAR

How! does he dissemble? Is he a hypocrite? Nay, then – 315
how – wife – sister, is he an hypocrite?

297 sd *doggedly* morosely
305 *communicated* had sexual intercourse
308 Possibly Pinchwife threatens to draw his sword again here, and at ll.
      347 and 364.

OLD LADY SQUEAMISH

 An hypocrite, a dissembler!   Speak, young harlotry, speak, how?

SIR JASPAR

 Nay, then – Oh, my head too! – Oh thou libidinous lady!

OLD LADY SQUEAMISH

 Oh thou harloting harlotry! Hast thou done't then?   320

SIR JASPAR

 Speak, good Horner, art thou a dissembler, a rogue? Hast thou –

HORNER

 Soh –

LUCY (*Apart to* HORNER)

 I'll fetch you off, and her too, if she will but hold her tongue.   325

HORNER (*Apart to* LUCY)

 Canst thou? I'll give thee –

LUCY (*To* PINCHWIFE)

 Pray, have but patience to hear me, sir, who am the unfortunate cause of all this confusion. Your wife is innocent, I only culpable; for I put her upon telling you all these lies concerning my mistress in order to the 330 breaking off the match between Master Sparkish and her, to make way for Master Harcourt.

SPARKISH

 Did you so, eternal rotten-tooth? Then it seems my mistress was not false to me, I was only deceived by you. Brother that should have been, now man of conduct, 335 who is a frank person now – to bring your wife to her lover – ha?

LUCY

 I assure you, sir, she came not to Master Horner out of love, for she loves him no more –

MRS PINCHWIFE

 Hold, I told lies for you, but you shall tell none for me, 340 for I do love Master Horner with all my soul, and nobody shall say me nay. Pray don't you go to make poor Master Horner believe to the contrary;   'tis

---

319 *my head* i.e., he begins to feel he is a cuckold

323 *soh* Possibly Horner sighs, like Mrs Pinchwife at IV.ii.130, though there Q1–5, O have a stage-direction.

324 *she* i.e., Mrs Pinchwife, who soon interrupts Lucy as we expect

335 *man of conduct* you who tell us how to conduct ourselves

336 *frank* i.e., Pinchwife's sarcasm (III.ii.360) is thrown back at him

spitefully done of you, I'm sure.

HORNER (*Aside to* MRS PINCHWIFE)

    Peace, dear idiot!   345

MRS PINCHWIFE

    Nay, I will not peace.

PINCHWIFE

    Not till I make you.

Enter DORILANT, QUACK

DORILANT

    Horner, your servant;   I am the doctor's guest, he must
    excuse our intrusion.

QUACK

    But what's the matter, gentlemen?   For heaven's sake, 350
    what's the matter?

HORNER

    Oh, 'tis well you are come.   'Tis a censorious world we
    live in;   you may have brought me a reprieve, or else I
    had   died   for   a   crime   I   never   committed,   and   these
    innocent ladies had suffered with me.   Therefore, pray 355
    satisfy these worthy, honourable, jealous gentlemen –
    that –   *Whispers*

QUACK

    Oh, I understand you;   is that all?   – Sir Jaspar, by
    heavens and upon the word of a physician sir –

                             Whispers to SIR JASPAR

SIR JASPAR

    Nay, I do believe you truly.   – Pardon me, my virtuous 360
    lady, and dear of honour.

OLD LADY SQUEAMISH

    What, then all's right again?

SIR JASPAR

    Ay, ay, and now let us satisfy him too.

                        They whisper with PINCHWIFE

PINCHWIFE

    An eunuch! Pray, no fooling with me.

QUACK

    I'll bring half the surgeons in town to swear it.   365

PINCHWIFE

    They!   – They'll swear a man that bled to death through

352 *censorious world* This echoes Lady Fidget's phrase at IV.iii.62.
354 *had* should have   361 *dear of honour* See II.i.412 note.
366–7 Doctors sometimes perjured themselves about the causes of deaths
    through duelling, as it was illegal.

his wounds died of an apoplexy.

QUACK

Pray hear me, sir. Why, all the town has heard the
report of him.

PINCHWIFE

But does all the town believe it?   370

QUACK

Pray enquire a little, and first of all these.

PINCHWIFE

I'm sure when I left the town he was the lewdest fellow
in't.

QUACK

I tell you, sir, he has been in France since; pray ask but
these ladies and gentlemen, your friend Master 375
Dorilant. – Gentlemen and ladies, ha'n't you all heard
the late sad report of poor Master Horner?

ALL LADIES

Ay, ay, ay.

DORILANT

Why, thou jealous fool, do'st thou doubt it? He's an
arrant French capon.   380

MRS PINCHWIFE

'Tis false, sir, you shall not disparage poor Master
Horner, for to my certain knowledge –

LUCY

Oh hold!

SQUEAMISH (*Aside to* LUCY)

Stop her mouth!

LADY FIDGET (*To* PINCHWIFE)

Upon my honour, sir, 'tis as true –   385

DAINTY

D'ye think we would have been seen in his company?

SQUEAMISH

Trust our unspotted reputations with him!

LADY FIDGET (*Aside to* HORNER)

This you get, and we too, by trusting your secret to a
fool.

HORNER

Peace, madam. (*Aside to* QUACK) Well, doctor, is not 390
this a good design, that carries a man on unsuspected,
and brings him off safe?

---

380   *capon* castrated cock, eunuch
385, 399 sp *LADY FIDGET* ed. (*Old. La. Fid.* Q1-5, O).

PINCHWIFE (*Aside*)

Well, if this were true; but my wife –

DORILANT *whispers with* MRS PINCHWIFE

ALITHEA

Come, brother, your wife is yet innocent you see. But have a care of too strong an imagination, lest like an over-concerned, timorous gamester, by fancying an unlucky cast, it should come. Women and fortune are truest still to those that trust 'em.

395

LUCY

And any wild thing grows but the more fierce and hungry for being kept up, and more dangerous to the keeper.

400

ALITHEA

There's doctrine for all husbands, Master Harcourt.

HARCOURT

I edify, madam, so much that I am impatient till I am one.

DORILANT

And I edify so much by example I will never be one.

405

SPARKISH

And because I will not disparage my parts I'll ne'er be one.

HORNER

And I, alas, can't be one.

PINCHWIFE

But I must be one – against my will, to a country wife, with a country murrain to me.

410

MRS PINCHWIFE (*Aside*)

And I must be a country wife still too, I find, for I can't, like a city one, be rid of my musty husband and do what I list.

HORNER

Now, sir, I must pronounce your wife innocent, though I blush whilst I do it, and I am the only man by her now

415

393 sd What do they whisper about? She perhaps tells him Horner is not impotent, and he perhaps tells her she can't marry Horner and must deceive Pinchwife.

403 *edify* profit spiritually from Alithea's 'doctrine'; a Puritan term, used with mock solemnity

406 sp SPARKISH Q2–5, O (*Eew.* Q1). The Q1 reading baffles all editors.
disparage my parts lower myself (by an unequal match); echoing what he said at II.i.289 but with a different meaning

410 *murrain* cattle plague; 'he talks as like a grazier as he looks', as mentioned at I.i.395

exposed to shame, which I will straight drown in wine,
as you shall your suspicion, and the ladies' troubles we'll
divert with a ballet. Doctor, where are your maskers?

LUCY

Indeed, she's innocent, sir, I am her witness. And her
end of coming out was but to see her sister's wedding,   420
and what she has said to your face of her love to Master
Horner was but the usual innocent revenge on a
husband's jealousy – was it not, madam? Speak.

MRS PINCHWIFE (*Aside to* LUCY *and* HORNER)

Since you'll have me tell more lies. – Yes, indeed, bud.

PINCHWIFE

For my own sake fain I would all believe;   425
Cuckolds like lovers should themselves deceive.
But – (*Sighs*) –
His honour is least safe, too late I find,
Who trusts it with a foolish wife or friend.

A dance of cuckolds

HORNER

Vain fops, but court, and dress, and keep a pother   430
To pass for women's men with one another;
But he who aims by women to be prized,
First by the men, you see, must be despised.

[*Exeunt*]

418 *ballet* dance in masquerade
Doctor, where are your maskers? Holger M. Klein suggests the question
should be put to Sir Jaspar, who promised 'fiddles' (V.ii.102), perhaps
implying masqueraders (*Archiv*, vol. 211 (1974), 66–8). But Sir Jaspar
would not have provided a *dance of cuckolds* (1. 429); Quack probably
would, and he and Horner seem to be plotting something at V.ii.110–11.
Such final dances were conventional in comedy and needed little
explanation.
420 *end of* purpose in
429 sd   The final dance does not express the harmony of conventional
comedy. Weales argues that if it is to have the effect of poking fun at
Pinchwife and Sir Jaspar it must be set to music associated with
cuckolds, and suggests the tune 'Cuckolds in a Row', which was readily
available in John Playford's *The Dancing Master*. But as Weales says,
Pepys saw Charles II dancing to this tune in December 1662; surely the
comic effect could have been achieved more reliably by having the
masqueraders wear horns.
430 *keep a pother* make a fuss
433 sd ed. Q1 does not have an *exeunt* here; it has '*FINIS*' lower down the
page, and 'FINIS' again after the epilogue on the next page. Many but
not all late seventeenth-century play quartos have an *exeunt* or *exeunt*

EPILOGUE

Spoken by Mrs Knepp

Now, you the vigorous, who daily here
O'er vizard-mask in public domineer,
And what you'd do to her if in place where;
Nay, have the confidence to cry 'Come out!'
Yet when she says 'Lead on' you are not stout;   5
But to your well-dressed brother straight turn round
And cry 'Pox on her, Ned, she can't be sound!'
Then slink away, a fresh one to engage,
With so much seeming heat and loving rage,
You'd frighten listening actress on the stage;   10
Till she at last has seen you huffing come
And talk of keeping in the tiring-room,
Yet cannot be provoked to lead her home.
Next, you Falstaffs of fifty, who beset
Your buckram maidenheads, which your friends get;   15
And whilst to them you of achievements boast,
They share the booty, and laugh at your cost.

---

omnes after the last line of the play and before the epilogue; but the stage
business is not obvious. At the end of *The Man of Mode* (1676) Old Bellair
says 'So now we'll in' and addresses '*to the pit*' a couplet requesting
applause; this is followed by an *exeunt omnes* and an epilogue. In Restoration productions generally the curtain was probably not lowered till after
the epilogue (Pierre Danchin, privately). So I suggest that in a modern
production of *The Country Wife* the players should all go off after Horner's
final speech, and come back for the applause; then the actress playing Lady
Fidget should step forward as herself, and speak the epilogue.

Mrs Knepp Q2–5, O (Mr *Hart* Q1). Obviously the epilogue should be
spoken by an actress.
2 *vizard-mask* See I.i.186 note.
3 *if in place where* if you were in a convenient place
4 '*Come out!*' Come out and fight
5 *stout* brave
7 *sound* See V.ii.47 note.
11 *huffing* See Prologue, l. 19 note.
12 *keeping* See I.i.460 note.
    tiring-room See Prologue, l. 25 note.
·14–17 These lines refer to *Henry IV, Part I* II.iv, where Falstaff boasts of
having fought numerous 'rogues in buckram suits' after the Gadshill
robbery, though he has in fact run away. His friends Prince Hal and
Poins have shared the booty and have the last laugh. Similarly elderly
gallants boast of their conquests to the young men who have actually had
the women.

In fine, you essenced boys, both old and young,
Who would be thought so eager, brisk, and strong,
Yet do the ladies, not their husbands, wrong;   20
Whose purses for your manhood make excuse,
And keep your Flanders mares for show, not use;
Encouraged by our woman's man today,
A Horner's part may vainly think to play;
And may intrigues so bashfully disown   25
That they may doubted be by few or none;
May kiss the cards at picquet, ombre, loo,
And so be thought to kiss the lady too;
But, gallants, have a care, faith, what you do.
The world, which to no man his due will give,   30
You by experience know you can deceive,
And men may still believe you vigorous,
But then we women – there's no coz'ning us!

FINIS

18 *essenced* perfumed
22 *Flanders mares* (literally) horses for the heavy coaches of the aristocracy, a
    status symbol; (metaphorically) kept women or prostitutes
24–6 i.e., the boys may pretend embarrassment in the hope of getting a false
    reputation for being rakes
27 *kiss the cards* i.e., make a flirtatious gesture
    piquet, ombre, loo fashionable card games
33 *coz'ning* cozening, deceiving